DramaScripts

Edited by

MARTIN LEWIS

JOHN RAINER

OXFORD
UNIVERSITY PRESS

OXFORD
UNIVERSITY PRESS

Great Clarendon Street, Oxford OX2 6DP

Oxford University Press is a department of the University of Oxford.
It furthers the University's objective of excellence in research,
scholarship, and education by publishing worldwide in

Oxford   New York

Auckland   Cape Town   Dar es Salaam   Hong Kong   Karachi
Kuala Lumpur   Madrid   Melbourne   Mexico City   Nairobi
New Delhi   Shanghai   Taipei   Toronto

With offices in

Argentina   Austria   Brazil   Chile   Czech Republic   France   Greece
Guatemala   Hungary   Italy   Japan   Poland   Portugal   Singapore
South Korea   Switzerland   Thailand   Turkey   Ukraine   Vietnam

Oxford is a registered trade mark of Oxford University Press
in the UK and in certain other countries

British Library Cataloguing in Publication Data

Data available

ISBN-13: 978-0-19-832180-4
ISBN-10: 0-19-832180-5

10 9 8 7 6 5 4 3 2 1

Printed and bound by Creative Print and Design Wales, Ebbw Vale.

Contents

Introduction

Welcome to *Oxford Dramascripts!*

Oxford Dramascripts are collections of thought-provoking extracts and short plays especially selected or commissioned to provide a source of fresh, relevant material that will meet the practical needs of all GCSE Drama students.

Each *Dramascripts* volume features ten scripts and covers a wide range of compelling themes and challenging issues. Cast sizes vary between three and eight actors and the scripts last between 15 and 40 minutes respectively, making them ideal for use in examined performance.

Every script is followed by a double-page spread of explorative, thought-provoking activities, carefully designed to tease out questions raised by the text and providing stimulating insights into the writing. The activities will act as a springboard for more detailed work on each piece and whet the appetite for further study.

In this volume, *Key Texts*, you will find ten extracts chosen with care from titles on set or recommended texts lists for GCSE Drama. The range, which features plays from different times and cultures, includes *East is East*, *Miss Julie*, *Metamorphosis* and *After Juliet* to name but four. Each piece is preceded by a cast list and brief outline of the whole plot, and provides inspiring opportunities both for study and performance.

East is East

Ayub Khan-Din

Characters in this extract

George	the Pakistani owner of a Salford fish and chip shop
Ella	George's British wife
Meenah	George and Ella's only daughter
Sajit	
Maneer	four of George and Ella's six sons
Tariq	
Abdul	
Mr Shah	father of two unattractive daughters, potential wives for two of George and Ella's sons
Annie	Ella's best friend

Plot summary

East is East is an autobiographical play which explores the trials and tribulations of George and Ella Khan as they raise seven rebellious children. George, the children's Pakistani father, is adamant that his children wed other Pakistanis, while Ella, George's British wife, would rather the children made their own choices. The central paradox that faces the Khan children is the fact that their own father has married someone outside his race.

In this extract, the Khan's prepare to receive a visitor: Mr Shah has two daughters and George hopes to arrange marriages for two of his six sons.

*The **Khans'** house, Sunday. **Ella** is plaiting **Meenah's** hair. **Sajit** sits oblivious to all the confusion around him, reading a comic.*

Meenah   Ouch! Mam, you're pulling me hair out.

Ella   Keep it bloody still then. Sajit – go upstairs and ask your Dad to give you the nit comb.

Sajit   I 'aven't got nits.

Ella   Well stop scratching your bleeding head. [*To **Maneer**.*] Are you out of that bath yet Maneer?

Maneer   I've not been in yet.

Ella   Well, don't bother, you haven't got time. Just have a quick wash.

Maneer   Oh mam I want a bath.

Ella   Alright. In and out quick. [*To **Meenah**.*] Did you use the big pan for the curry like I told you?

Meenah   Yeah, and I got some more chappati flour mam as well. Will you tell Maneer to help with the chappatis mam?

Sajit   I can make chappatis mam.

Ella   You don't go near that flour with those hands.

Sajit   Why can't I?

Meenah   'Cos we'll all end up with scabs you mong!

*Enter **Tariq** and **Abdul**.*

Tariq   Mam – I can't do this tie.

Ella   Hang on, I haven't got two pairs of hands. Abdul! Fix Tariq's tie. [*Pause.*] Where's Saleem?

Tariq	He said he was gonna pick his model up. Mam, this tie's not right.
Ella	Come here. [*She does* **Tariq's** *tie*] There, that'll do. [*She strokes his hair,* **Meenah** *and* **Abdul** *exchange looks.*] Go on get lost.
Ella	Sajit go upstairs and ask your dad to get me jewellery out of the safe. [*As* **Sajit** *goes.*] And take that bleeding parka off! Abdul, get the posh cups out of the cabinet in the kitchen.
Meenah	I don't know why they can't have mugs like everyone else, they only slurp it out of the saucers.
Ella	Well if he does don't look, I'm not having you lot laughing and showing me up. Right, Meenah veil on! Tariq, Abdul, let's have a look at you, you'll do. Maneer!
	Manner appears from the kitchen, **Ella** *looks at him.*
Ella	Brylcreem!
Meenah	I feel stupid in this.
	Sajit enters.
Sajit	You look it.
Meenah	Shut your gob, or I'll shut it for you.
Ella	If I catch you fighting in that sari, I'll wipe the floor with both of you. Now go and get me some fags from Butterworths.
Meenah	No way, I'm not going out dressed like this.
Ella	Sajit go and get me twenty Park Drive. Maneer, have you emptied that bath out?
Maneer	Yeah, can you get zinc poisoning from it mam?
Ella	Don't be so bleeding stupid.
Meenah	I wish we had a proper one, that one don't half scratch your arse.
	Meenah gets a clip round the ear from **Ella***.*
Ella	Hey, gob-shite, I've told you once, keep it shut. We've got visitors.

Sajit bursts in.

Sajit   Mam, quick, the Paki's here!

Ella   Oh for Jesus sake. Abdul, muzzle him will you.

Abdul   Sajit, get over here!

Mr Shah enters greeted by **Ella**. **Ella** leads him into the parlour, followed by the **Others**, **Sajit** bringing up the rear trying to see. **Ella** has now got her slightly posh voice on. Mr Shah has with him two large photographs, in ornate frames, of his daughters.

George   [off] Ella, this is Mr Shah.

Mr Shah   Asalaam-a-lekum.

Ella   Walekum-a-salaam. Would you like to come through to the parlour Mr Shah?

Meenah   [to **Tariq**] What's she talking like that for?

George introduces the boys to **Mr Shah**.

George   This is my son Abdul.

Mr Shah   Asalaam-a-lekum.

Abdul   Walekum-a-salaam.

George   Tariq.

Mr Shah   Aslaam-a-lekum.

Tariq   Walekum-a-salaam.

George   Maneer.

Mr Shah   Asalaam-a-lekum.

Maneer   Walekum-a-salaam.

Ella   [calls] Meenah. [Enter **Meenah**.] Would you bring in the tea luv?

George   This is my daughter Meenah.

Meenah   [posh] Righty-ho. [She goes out to fetch the tea.]

Pause.

Ella   Did you find it alright?

Mr Shah   Oh yes, no problem.

Pause.

You have a very nice family, all boys, this is very good. God has blessed you.

Ella   Well I could have done without so much blessing.

Mr Shah   I'm sorry?

Ella   Doesn't matter. [*Changing the subject.*] Lovely frames you've got there.

Mr Shah   Yes, let me show you, these are my daughters, Nigget and Afsal-jaan. [*He passes them over, they're quite heavy.*]

Ella   Oh they're quite hefty... the frames I mean! Look, George, aren't they lovely?

Sajit   Which one's Tariq's?

Ella   Sit down cock, over there by the door.

George   Very nice photo. Where you buy frame like this?

Mr Shah   We had them especially made for our girls, gold leaf you know.

*Enter **Meenah** with the tea, she sees the photos. She can barely control her laughter, this could be dangerous. She scuttles out of the room quick.*

Meenah   I'll just go and get the biscuits. [*She almost snorts this.*]

***Tariq** and **Abdul** hear this but **Ella** kills another outbreak with a look.*

Mr Shah   Do all your sons live at home?

***Ella** lights a fag. **Mr Shah** looks on disapprovingly.*

Ella   All except Nazir, he's the eldest.

George   He travelling salesman.

***Sajit** moves closer to **Mr Shah**, he does a large twitch.*

Mr Shah   Erm. And this must be your youngest. [*To* **Sajit**] And how old are you?

Sajit   Not old enough to get married, so don't ask me.

George   [*veiled threat*] Sajit puther, go see if Saleem here yet.

Mr Shah   Ah yes, Saleem your college student, the engineer.

Sajit   He's not, he's an artist, I've got a picture he drew of a...

Sajit is about to take out the picture **Saleem** *drew of a foreskin.* **Maneer** *retrieves it just in time.*

Abdul   He means engineer... who erm paints engines Mr Shah...

Ella   Sajit. Saleem. Now. [**Sajit** *gets the message and goes.*] Sorry about that Mr Shah he's erm... just been circumcised...

Mr Shah   Indeed.

Ella   Where's that Meenah with them biscuits?

Tariq   Shall I put the pictures of your daughters on the radiogram Mr Shah?

Mr Shah   So Tariq, do you have hobbies?

George   Only good ones. He like to work in shop most time.

Enter **Meenah** *with biscuits.*

Meenah   Would you like a biscuit, Mr Shah?

Mr Shah   Where did you get this sari?

Meenah   Me Auntie Riffat in Pakistan.

Mr Shah   This is not what our women wear. You should wear Shalwar kameeze. It will look much better on you than this thing.

Ella   Her Auntie Riffat said all women wear saris in Islamabad, and she's quite well to do, isn't she George.

George   Riffat bloody stupy. [*To* **Mr Shah.**] Even in Pakistan women getting too bloody moderns.

Mr Shah   It's the government people I blame. They should set an example to the country.

Ella   I think it looks lovely.

Mr Shah   It is not traditional dress in Pakistan.

George   Tradition see, Ella.

Annie   [off] Youuu! Only me!

Annie pokes her head round the door.

Annie   Oh, I didn't know you had visitors. I won't stay long.

George   Annie, this is my friend Mr Shah, he daughters go be marry Abdul and Tariq.

Annie   Congratulations Mr Shah. [*Notices the pictures.*] Are these 'em? Oh, they look bleedin' gorgeous, you're lucky you two, landing a couple of belters like that.

George   [*To Mr Shah.*] Annie working for me since we first getting shop.

Ella   I suppose you'll want tea now?

Annie   Seeing as you've asked me so bleeding politely I will.

Ella   Meenah go and put the kettle on.

Meenah exits.

Annie   Yeah they're lovely them, Mr Shah, you must be very proud of them. Beltin' frames as well.

Mr Shah   Yes, gold leaf you know.

Annie   I do know, I got something similar meself off the docks.

Ella   [*trying to shut her up.*] Do you want a biscuit?

Annie   No ta. Three bob the pair they were. I've got a view of Kinder Scout in one and a three-dimensional of our lady in the other, looks beltin' don't it Ella?

Mr Shah   Mrs Khan...

Ella   Call me Ella.

Annie   Everybody does.

Mr Shah   Erm... Mrs Khan. I am very proud that your sons are joining my family. [*This* *makes **Ella** sit up and take note, even she knows it's the girls who are joining her family.*] I can see you have brought them up to be very respectful, which is very difficult in this day and age.

Annie   You're right there Mr Shah, they're a credit to her, and you George.

George   Oh yes, they good boys, no bring a trouble.

Annie   They'll do owt for you these two, you know last Whitsun they carried the banner of the Sacred Heart at a moment's notice, all the way from Regent Road t' town hall in Albert Square and back.

Mr Shah   What banner is this?

Annie   For the Whit week walks. Abdul and Tariq on the banner, Saleem, Maneer and our Clifford holding ribbons from the model of the holy sepulchre, with Sajit and Meenah chuckin' petals about in front.

George   Ella, what she bloody talking about?

Mr Shah   [*slightly perturbed*] Is this a religious ceremony?

Annie   In a way I suppose you could say it was, but hardly anyone round 'ere's religious. It's just a day out f' kids and a new set of clothes.

Abdul   We just helped out that once, lucky we were all there really.

Lights up on living room.

Meenah   Brew up Twitch.

Sajit   Get stuffed you fat cow!

Meenah   I'll stuff you, you little twat!

***Meenah** flings herself and her sari over the sofa and onto **Sajit**. He screams.*

Up on the parlour.

Ella   Well you've got to lend a hand haven't you, I mean that's how we brought them up.

Mr Shah   But this was not their religion.

Annie	[*digging herself out*] Well that what a couple of belters you're getting, Mr Shah, they just jumped in there and gave help where help was needed, good Samaritans they were, just like in the bible when…

*We hear **Sajit** scream. This is a good time for **Ella** to cut **Annie** off before she puts her foot in it again.*

Ella	Tariq cock, will you go and see what they're up to? [*To **Mr Shah**].* Kids eh? Were your two like that when they were younger?

Tariq *exits.*

Mr Shah	No, my wife was a schoolmistress, she's always believed in firm discipline. Especially in a non-Pakistani environment.
Ella	Oh I think you can be too harsh, don't you Annie?
Annie	Oh aye, yeah, mind you, our Peter knows how far he can go, before I knock him to kingdom come – and that's just me husband Mr Shah!

*She bursts into laughter, **Ella** also but not as much as she would like. **George** and **Mr Shah** do not find it funny.*

Annie	Do you smoke Mr Shah? [*He declines, she gives one to **Ella**.*] You could even say that in a Pakistani environment you'd still have to know where to draw the line with them, whereas with Ella and George they didn't have that environment, so they had to find their own line here in Salford, in this area among non-Pakistanis, but even without other Pakistanis they've got what you have as well, and done very well with it… like you have done. [*She's got to get out this.*] You know they look just like you Mr Shah. [*Indicates the photos.*]
Mr Shah	Oh, no, no.
Ella	She's right Mr Shah. They've got your eyebrows.
Mr Shah	I think there is a great preponderance placed on looks.
Annie	A what sorry?
George	'Ponderance. [*To **Mr Shah**.*] What is the latest news from East Pakistan?

Lights up on living room.

Meenah   Have you seen them pictures though!

Tariq   The one in the red looked like she had a hair-line that started from here eyebrows.

Meenah   At least she had a neck. Our Abdul's looked like Smiffy out of the Bash Street Kids!

Enter Maneer with a teapot.

Maneer   Me mam said to hurry up with that tea.

Tariq   What's going on in there?

Maneer   Me dad's building up to the war.

Up on the parlour.

George   Is bloody Indians see!

Annie   I'd better be going, got to go and see the undertaker about Scots Bertha, see you later George. Nice to meet you Mr Shah.

Ella   See you later. [**Annie** *exits.*]

Mr Shah   [*to* **George**] General Yahya Khan will hold the country together.

George   Ah yes, he's the man for that...

Ella   [*trying to make conversation*] Do your family come from Azad Kashmir, Mr Shah?

Mr Shah   My wife's family, mine are from Lahore, a beautiful city, the home of the arts in Pakistan. Have you been to Pakistan Mrs Khan?

Ella   Never been asked.

Mr Shah   But you must go on holiday sometime, two months at least, see the whole country.

Ella   Yeah, well, we can only manage two weeks in Rhyl. Even then George has to stay home and mind the shop.

Mr Shah   Really... well Pakistan is very different to Rhyl.

Ella   Yeah right... it's got the sun for a start... have you been in England long Mr Shah?

Mr Shah   Since 1949. My wife studied here, in London, but later returned when my daughters were very young. I don't think this is a fit society to bring up girls.

Ella   All depends how you bring them up I think.

Mr Shah   But you have experienced only boys Mrs. Khan.

Ella   I've got Meenah as well Mr Shah.

Mr Shah   Yes this is true Mrs. Khan but… our girls are different.

Ella   [*does not like this.*] Really.

George   Han, this is true, too much tickle-tackle go on see. You go to town, and you bloody see all bloody Indian girl. All bloody up to tickle-tackle with boy.

Mr Shah   This is the problem with our community, they don't realise what a great danger is to leave your children to grow up in this country.

George   I been in this country since 1930, an' I telling you no even bloody English same.

Ella   What sort of work did you do when you first came Mr Shah?

Mr Shah   Very degrading work I assure you Mrs Khan, very degrading. I was over-qualified you see. First I swept the floor in a mill, then I worked on the buses. Now I have four butchers shops, two cars and a semi-detached house in Trafford Park.

Ella   Really?

Mr Shah   With double extensions.

Ella   That's nice and roomy for you. Abdul go and see where that tea is will you.

Mr Shah   My daughters both have their own bedrooms you know. With Axminster carpet.

Ella   Nice.

Mr Shah   They have attached bathrooms with same carpet. My wife's idea.

Ella   I've always found oil cloth better for the bathroom, stops that smell of damp.

George   We have bathroom soon I think.

Mr Shah   How do you manage with so little room and so many children Mrs Khan? It must be a bit of a squeeze.

Ella   I've got three double beds and one single for Meenah.

Mr Shah   But where do you propose to put my daughters?

Ella   One in the attic, the other on top of the chippy with Abdul.

Mr Shah   [*making his move*] But we have so much room at our house, it seems such a shame to waste it. Would it not be more convenient if your sons were to move in with us?

He looks to **George** *for agreement.*

Ella   Erm. I thought the daughters-in-law moved in with their husband's family.

Mr Shah   But my daughters are used to modern conveniences. Perhaps when you get your bathroom fitted they may be able to move back. Though I'd have thought you'd be grateful for the extra space, I know I would be.

Ella   But you don't know what you'd be getting yourself into Mr Shah. You've never experienced boys have you?

Context of the play

The play is set in Salford in the 1970s. The Khans are a truly multicultural family: Ella, the mother, is white, and George, the father, is a Pakistani fish-and-chip-shop owner concerned with bringing up his family according to Muslim tradition. The children living at home are aged from 12 to 23 years (the eldest son lives away, having already been disowned by his father). They all respond differently to their father's attempts to influence them – and to the contradictory values of the society in which they live.

This extract starts with the family preparing for a visit from Mr Shah, a local businessman, who has two daughters of a similar age to Abdul and Tariq, the Khans' sons. George has arranged marriages on their behalf and will not listen to the protestations of his family.

Much of the comedy in the scene derives from the Khan parents' efforts to keep up appearances in order to impress Mr Shah, in spite of the anarchic behaviour of the family. A visit from Annie, Ella's sister, only makes things worse.

Introductory task

1. In your group, make a spider diagram which records your responses to the idea of 'marriage'. Once complete, create a sequence of still images of family 'wedding portraits' based on what you have written.

2. Choose one of the portraits, then create a time-line of key moments leading up to it. For each key moment create two contrasting still images: the 'ideal' and the 'reality'. As a final task, find words spoken in the extract from East is East that might fit the images you have created, or can be spoken as captions.

Task 1

1. As the extract progresses, Ella, who already had some doubts about the wedding, begins to alter her viewpoint. Select three key moments and create tableaux which demonstrate Ella's changing attitude to Mr Shah. Is there a particular moment which is the turning point in her understanding?

2. Once the tableaux have been created, hold the images and run the dialogue from those moments in the play. Using another student, 'thought tap' the

character of Ella at those moments. This means voicing her unheard thoughts, which might contradict what she says, to illustrate the sub-text.

Task 2

This extract ends before the scene's climax. What do you predict might happen? Improvise a possible ending for the scene. Start the next scene with a still image illustrating the final words of the extract.

Task 3

Tanika Gupta's adaptation of Harold Brighouse's *Hobson's Choice* is another play about a British Asian family, also set in Salford (see page 40).

1. Read this extract. You will find that it parallels *East is East* in a number of ways, not least in the central theme of an oppressive patriarch's effect on his family. But its style, particularly the language used by the characters, is very different.

2. In both plays there is a strong central female character – here, Ella, in *Hobson's Choice*, Durga. Set up a 'chat show' where they and other family members talk about their lives, ambitions and attitudes to marriage.

Cultural references

Research the customs associated with marriage in different cultures. How far do you feel that the romantic idea of 'love and marriage', so important in the West, is the best basis for stable and long-lasting relationships?

Writing task

1. Create a sequence of director's notes for the scene giving advice to the actor playing Ella. Consider her changing attitude to Mr Shah, outlined in Task 1 above. How should she show this through voice, gesture and body language?

2. Script a short scene between Abdul and Tariq which takes place in private, when they are first told about the arranged marriage. Try to portray the boys' mixed feelings – loyalty to their father and their family, contrasted with their need to be independent and make their own decisions.

The Resistable Rise of Arturo Ui

Bertolt Brecht

Characters in this extract

Arturo Ui	gang leader
Giuseppe Givola	the florist and a ganster
an Actor	
First Bodyguard	
Second Bodyguard	

Plot summary

The Resistible Rise of Arturo Ui was written in exile in 1941, just before Brecht's arrival in the USA. The play is a savage and witty parable of the rise of Hitler, period which Brecht describes with powerful satire.

While Brecht recasts Hitler as Arturo Ui, a small-time Chicago gangster who is taking over the city's greengrocery trade, each scene is preceded by a sign linking the events in Germany and those taking place in the play. These signs make the symbolism extremely evident.

In this extract, Ui takes acting lessons to improve his pronunciation and body language.

Hotel Mammoth. **Ui's** *suite.* *Two bodyguards lead a ragged actor to* **Ui**. *In the background* **Givola**.

First Bodyguard   It's an actor, boss. Unarmed.

Second Bodyguard   He can't afford a rod. He was able to get tight because they pay him to declaim in the saloons when they're tight. But I'm told that he's good. He's one of them classical guys.

Ui   Okay. Here's the problem. I've been given to understand that my pronunciation leaves something to be desired. It looks like I'm going to have to say a word or two on certain occasions, especially when I get into politics, so I've decided to take lessons. The gestures too.

The Actor   Very well.

Ui   Get the mirror.

A bodyguard comes front stage with a large standing mirror.

Ui   First the walk. How do you guys walk in the theatre or the opera?

The Actor   I see what you mean. The grand style. Julius Caesar, Hamlet, Romeo – that's Shakespeare. Mr Ui, you've come to the right man. Old Mahonney can teach you the classical manner in ten minutes. Gentlemen, you see before you a tragic figure. Ruined by Shakespeare. An English poet. If it weren't for Shakespeare, I could be on Broadway right now. The tragedy of a character. 'Don't play Shakespeare when you're playing Ibsen, Mahonney! Look at the calendar! This is 1912, sir!' – 'Art knows no calendar, sir!' say I. 'And art is my life.' Alas.

Givola   I think you've got the wrong guy, boss. He's out of date.

Ui   We'll see about that. Walk around like they do in this Shakespeare.

The actor *walks around.*

Ui   Good!

Givola   You can't walk like that in front of cauliflower men. It ain't natural.

Ui   What do you mean it ain't natural? Nobody's natural in this day and age. When I walk I want people to know I'm walking.

He copies **the actor's** *gait.*

The Actor Head back. [**Ui** *throws his head back*] The foot touches the ground toe first. [**Ui's** *foot touches the ground toe first*] Good. Excellent. You have a natural gift. Only the arms. They're not quite right. Stiff. Perhaps if you joined your arms in front of your private parts. [**Ui** *joins his arms in front of his private parts*] Not bad. Relaxed but firm. But head back. Good. Just the right gait for your purposes, I believe, Mr Ui. What else do you wish to learn?

Ui How to stand. In front of people.

Givola Have two big bruisers right behind you and you'll be standing pretty.

Ui That's bunk. When I stand I don't want people looking at the two bozoes behind me. I want them looking at me. Correct me!

He takes a stance, his arms crossed over his chest.

The Actor A possible solution. But common. You don't want to look like a barber, Mr Ui. Fold your arms like this. [*He folds his arms in such a way that the backs of his hands remain visible. His palms are resting on his arms not far from the shoulder*] A trifling change, but the difference is incalculable. Draw the comparison in the mirror, Mr Ui.

Ui tries out the new position before the mirror.

Ui Not bad.

Givola What's all this for, boss? Just for those Fancy-pants in the Trust?

Ui Hell, no! It's for
The little people. Why, for instance, do
You think this Clark makes such a show of grandeur?
Not for his peers. His bank account
Takes care of them, the same as my big bruisers
Lend me prestige in certain situations.
Clark makes a show of grandeur to impress
The little man. I mean to do the same.

Givola But some will say is doesn't look inborn.
Some people stick at that.

Ui I know they do.
But I'm not trying to convince professors

	And smart-Alecks. My object is the little
	Man's image of his master.

Givola   Don't overdo
The master, boss. Better the democrat.
The friendly, reassuring type in shirtsleeves.

Ui   I've got old Dogsborough for that.

Givola   His image
Is kind of tarnished, I should say. He's still
An asset on the books, a venerable
Antique. But people aren't as eager as they
Were to exhibit him. They're not so sure
He's genuine. It's like the family Bible
Nobody opens any more since, piously
Tuning the yellowed pages with a group
Of friends, they found a dried-out bedbug. But
Maybe he's good enough for Cauliflower.

Ui   I decide who's respectable.

Givola   Sure thing, boss.
There's nothing wrong with Dogsborough. We can
Still use him. They haven't even dropped him
At City Hall. The crash would be too loud.

Ui   Sitting.

The Actor   Sitting. Sitting is almost the hardest, Mr Ui. There are men who can walk;
there are men who can stand; but find me a man who can sit. Take a chair
with a backrest, Mr Ui. But don't lean against it. Hands on thighs, to
abdomen, elbows away from body. How long can you sit like that, Mr Ui?

Ui   As long as I please.

The Actor   Then everything's perfect, Mr Ui.

Givola   You know, boss, when old Dogsborough passes on
Giri could take his place. He's got the
Popular touch. He plays the funny man
And laughs so loud in season that the plaster

Comes tumbling from the ceiling. Sometimes, though
He does it out of season, as for instance
When you step forward as the modest son of
The Bronx you really were and talk about
Those seven determined youngsters.

Ui   Then he laughs?

Givola   The plaster tumbles from the ceiling. Don't
Tell him I said so or he'll think I've got
It in for him. But maybe you could make
Him stop collecting hats.

Ui   What kind of hats?

Givola   The hats of people he's rubbed out. And running
Around with them in public. It's disgusting.

Ui   Forget it. I would never think of muzzling
The ox that treads my corn. I overlook
The petty foibles of my underlings.

To **the actor**.

And now to speaking! Speak a speech for me!

The Actor   Shakespeare. Nothing else. Julius Caesar. The Roman hero. [*He draws a little book from his pocket*] What do you say to Mark Antony's speech? Over Caesar's body. Against Brutus. The ringleader of Casear's assassins. A model of demagogy. Very famous. I played Antony in Zenith in 1908. Just what you need, Mr Ui. [*He takes a stance and recites Mark Antony's speech line for line.*]
Friends, Romans, countrymen, lend me your ears!

Reading from the little book, **Ui** *speaks the lines after him. Now and then* **the actor** *corrects him, but in the main* **Ui** *keeps his rough staccato delivery.*

The Actor   I come to bury Caesar, not to praise him.
The evil that men do lives after them;
The good is oft interred with their bones;
So let it be with Caesar. The noble Brutus
Hath told you Caesar was ambitious.

If it were so, it was a grievous fault,
And grievously hath Caesar answer'd it.

Ui   *continues by himself:*
Here, under leave of Brutus and the rest —
For Brutus is an honourable man;
So are they all, all honourable men —
Come I to speak in Caesar's funeral.
He was my friend, faithful and just to me;
But Brutus says he was ambitious;
And Brutus is an honourable man.
He hath brought many captives home to Rome,
Whose ransoms did the general coffers fill;
Did this in Caesar seem ambitious?
When that the poor have cried, Caesar hath wept;
Ambition should be made of sterner stuff.
Yet Brutus says he was ambitious;
And Brutus is an honourable man.
You all did see that on the Lupercal
I thrice presented him a kingly crown,
Which he did thrice refuse. Was this ambition?
Yet Brutus says he was ambitious;
And sure he is an honourable man.
I speak not to disprove what Brutus spoke,
But here I am to speak what I do know.
You all did love him once, not without cause?
What cause withholds you then, to mourn for him?

During the last lines the curtain slowly falls. A sign appears.

Context of the play

The Resistible Rise of Arturo Ui was first written in 1941, during the Second World War, while Bertolt Brecht was in exile from the Nazis. Brecht wrote a number of anti-Nazi plays during this period, and the rise of Arturo Ui – a gangster 'muscling in' on the Chicago greengrocery trade – parallels that of Hitler.

The play is in *parable* form – it is meant to serve as satirical attack on Hitler and his regime as well as a warning against fascism. Characters in the play are direct parallels of real historical figures: Dogsborough represents Chancellor Hindenberg, who eventually appointed Hitler as his successor in 1933, and Givola is the faithful Goebbels, whom Hitler appointed his Minister of Enlightenment and Propaganda upon coming to power. The play takes Shakespeare's *Richard III* as one of its models, but Brecht also uses references to *Julius Caesar* and gangster movies and employs a wide range of stylistic devices – captions, narration and songs – to make a powerful, highly comic play.

In the extract, Ui, aware that he will need to be more statesmanlike if he is to gain influence and power, has hired an out-of-work actor to advise him on public speaking. Givola, Ui's right hand man, is keen that Ui should seek to influence the powerful Cauliflower Trust if he is to gain power. Ui, however, recognizes that he needs to impress 'the little man'.

Introductory task

1. Write down your initial impressions of the scene and anything that you are unsure of or don't understand. Check these with your teacher.

2. Select three significant moments. Create still images of them, adding captions from the text if appropriate. Share your work with other groups and justify your selection.

Task 1

Adolf Hitler was a powerful public speaker noted for his ferocious declamatory style and his effect on huge crowds of people.

1. In this scene the Actor gives advice to Ui concerning his walk, stance, sitting position and voice. Read this part of the text. Create the positions suggested.

2. Using the Internet or reference books, collect images of Adolf Hitler appearing in public. Take note of his gestures and body language. Select the images of Hitler that most closely relate to the Actor's advice. Create a portfolio of still images that might be used to advise an actor playing the part of Ui in the scene.

Task 2

1. In the scene we see the figure of Hitler being 'constructed' before us. As the Actor demonstrates, a hesitant Ui copies, slowly gaining confidence until he 'emerges' during the final Mark Antony speech. What we are presented with is Ui/Hitler 'performing' the Shakespeare text, as a 'rehearsal' for what is to follow. How might this foreshadowing be suggested in the setting for the scene?

2. Create an insignia for Ui and his 'cauliflower gangsters' as they rise to power.

3. Using stage blocks, create a simple setting for the final speech, decorating it using your insignia. In your setting, try to hint at the sinister events that follow Ui's finding of his voice; it may be helpful to research the 'sets' used by the Nazis to create platforms for Hitler's own speech-making.

Cultural references

Find as many references as you can to politicians or other people (fictional or real) who have 'reinvented' themselves to achieve their goals. For example:

Margaret Thatcher   Michael Jackson
Eliza Doolittle (in *Pygmalion/My Fair Lady*) David Beckham.

Why might actors be good people to consult in these situations?

Research the life and work of Bertolt Brecht (1899–1956), and in particular his use of *alienation effects* in his *epic theatre*.

Writing task

Create some notes giving advice to the actor playing Ui as he performs the 'Mark Antony' speech. What is the main challenge for the actor performing this speech? What effect should the transformation of Ui have on the audience? How should the actor play the scene to achieve this?

Miss Julie

August Strindberg

Characters in this extract

Miss Julie	the play's 25-year-old tragic heroine
Jean	the 30-year-old valet at Julie's family home
Christine	the 35-year-old family cook, and Jean's fiancée

Plot summary

It is Midsummer's Eve and celebrations are in full swing. Miss Julie, a headstrong young aristocrat seduces her father's valet, Jean. Jean's own fiancée, Christine, the cook, is unaware what is happening: she is asleep in the kitchen.

Jean suggests to Julie that they flee to escape the gossips, but is put off when Julie points out that she has no money. After heated discussion, he nevertheless repeats the suggestion and Julie goes to pack. Meanwhile, Jean confesses his infidelity to Christine, who is disgusted.

Julie returns with her canary, which she hopes to take along. Jean, however, kills the bird and Julie decides to stay and tell her father everything. When she changes her mind again, Christine promises to prevent any departures. Desperate, Julie asks Jean what to do. He tells her to take her own life and Julie leaves the room to obey him.

Jean [*enters alone*] She really *is* wild. The way she dances! And the people stand there sneering at her behind her back. Can you believe it, Christine?

Christine Poor thing. She's always a bit strange, when she's got her period. [*Intimately*] But won't he come and dance with me now?

Jean You're not angry with me for letting you down, are you?

Christine No! A little thing like that doesn't worry me. He knows that. Besides, I know my place ...

Jean [*puts his hand round her waist*] You are a sensible girl, Christine, you'll make a good wife ...

Miss Julie [*comes in. She's unpleasantly surprised: she speaks with forced gaiety*] Very gracious running away from your partner like that!

Jean On the contrary, Miss Julie, I ran back to the partner I left behind.

Miss Julie You dance like no one else do you know that? But why do you wear livery on Midsummer's Eve? Take it off at once!

Jean Then I must ask her ladyship to leave the kitchen for a moment because my black coat is over here. [*He points to the right and crosses*]

Miss Julie Are you embarrassed in front of me? Just to change a coat? Go into your room, then, and change there! Or stay here and I'll turn my back.

Jean With your permission, my lady! [*Goes to the right: we see his arm when he changes his coat.*]

Miss Julie [*to* **Christine**] Christine, are you actually engaged to Jean? He is very familiar with you.

Christine Engaged? Yes, if you like, that's what we call it.

Miss Julie Call it?

Christine Well, Miss Julie herself was engaged once and ...

Miss Julie Yes, but we were properly engaged ...

Christine Nothing came of it, though.

Jean comes in wearing a different coat.

Miss Julie Très gentil, Monsieur Jean, très gentil!

Jean Vous voulez plaisanter, Madame.

Miss Julie Et vous voulez parler français. Where did you learn that?

Jean In Switzerland, when I was the wine waiter: the 'sommelier' in one of the biggest hotels in Luzern.

Miss Julie You really look like a gentleman in that hunting jacket. Charmant! [*She sits down at the table.*]

Jean Forgive me, but that sounds patronising.

Miss Julie [hurt] Patronising?

Jean My natural modesty forbids me to believe that you would pay genuine compliments to someone in my position. I therefore have allowed myself to assume that you were flattering me or, to be more correct, were patronising me.

Miss Julie Where did you learn to speak like that? You must have been to the theatre.

Jean I've been to many theatres – here and abroad.

Miss Julie But you were born in this area, weren't you?

Jean My father was a hired labourer on the Attorney's estate next door. I used to see you as a child, you didn't notice me though.

Miss Julie No, really.

Jean Yes, really. And I remember in particular once ... no, I don't want to talk about that.

Miss Julie Oh! Tell me! Please? Just this once.

Jean No, I really don't want to now! Another time perhaps ...

Miss Julie Another time may never come. Why is it so dangerous now?

Jean It isn't dangerous. I just don't want to, that's all. Look at that one! [*He points at* **Christine** *who has fallen asleep in a chair by the stove.*]

Miss Julie She'll make a good wife, that one! Does she snore as well?

Jean She doesn't snore, but she talks in her sleep.

Miss Julie How do you know she talks in her sleep?

Jean I've heard it.

Pause, during which they look at each other.

Miss Julie Why don't you sit down?

Jean I couldn't allow myself to sit down in your presence.

Miss Julie But if I command you to?

Jean Then I'll obey.

Miss Julie Sit down then. No, wait. Could you give me something to drink first?

Jean I don't know what there is. Only beer, I think.

Miss Julie What do you mean, 'only beer'? My taste is very simple, I prefer it to wine.

Jean takes a bottle of beer from the cooler and opens it. He takes a glass and a plate out of the cupboard and serves her.

Jean Please, allow me.

Miss Julie Thank you. Won't you have a drink?

Jean I'm not so fond of beer myself, but if Miss Julie commands me to drink it.

Miss Julie Commands? Surely a gentleman should keep his lady company?

Jean Yes, he should.

Miss Julie Drink to my health then.

Jean hesitates.

I really believe the big boy is shy.

Jean kneels down with mock gallantry and raises his glass.

Jean Your good health, Ma'am.

Miss Julie And now: kiss my shoe!

Jean hesitates but then boldly seizes her foot, which he kisses lightly.

Miss Julie Excellent! I can see you've been to the theatre.

Jean Please let's stop this, Miss Julie, someone might come in and see us.

Miss Julie Does it matter?

Jean People would talk. It's as simple as that. If only you knew how their tongues were wagging up there just now.

Miss Julie What were they saying then? Tell me. Sit down.

Jean [*sits*] I don't want to hurt you, but they were insinuating ... well, you can guess! You are not a child. When people see a lady late at night, drinking alone with a man – even though he is a servant – then ...

Miss Julie Then what? Anyway, we are not alone. Christine is here.

Jean Sleeping.

Miss Julie Then I'll wake her up. [*She gets up.*] Christine are you asleep?

Christine [*in her sleep*] Bla bla bla bla.

Miss Julie Christine! God, I wish I could sleep like that.

Christine [*in her sleep*] The Count's boots have been polished – put the coffee on – at once, at once, at once, ha ha pah!

Miss Julie [*takes her by the nose*] Wake up!

Jean 'Golden slumbers fill your eyes.
Smiles awake you when you rise.'

Miss Julie [*sharply*] What?

Jean Some people slave over a hot stove all day long. Some people are tired at the end of the day. Sleep should be respected.

Miss Julie [*changes her tone*] That's ... you're right. [*She stretches her hand to* **Jean**.] Now come outside and pick some lilacs for me.

Jean   With her Ladyship?

Miss Julie With me!

Jean   Impossible! Absolutely not!

Miss Julie What do you mean? Surely you don't imagine ...

Jean   No, not me, but them –

Miss Julie What? That I am in love with the footman?

Jean   I am not a conceited man but things like that do happen and nothing is sacred to them.

Miss Julie You feel quite above then, don't you?

Jean   I am quite above them.

Miss Julie I can come down and ...

Jean   Don't come down Miss Julie, take my advice. No one will believe that you came down out of your own free will; the people will always say that you fell down.

Miss Julie I have more faith in the people than you do. Come and see. Come.

        She fixes him with her eyes – like a hawk fixes his prey.

Jean   You are strange. D'you know that?

Miss Julie Maybe! But so are you! Anyway everything is strange. Life, human beings, everything is a mess that's floating, floating across the water until it sinks, sinks! I have a recurring dream from time to time: I'm on top of a pillar. I'm sitting there, and I see no possible way of getting down. I feel dizzy when I look down but I know I must get down. I haven't got the courage to throw myself. I can't hold on. I long to be able to just fall but I don't fall. I know I won't have any peace until I'm down, no rest until I'm down, down to the ground. I also know that once I am down I'll want the ground to open and for me to sink, sink ... Have you ever felt anything like that?

Jean   No. I dream that I am lying underneath a tall tree in a dark forest. I want to get up up to the top and look around me across the bright landscape where the sun shines. I want to plunder the bird's nest up there with the golden eggs. I climb and climb but the trunk is so thick and slippery and it's so far to the first branch. I know that if I could only reach that first branch I could climb up to the top step by step. I haven't reached it yet but I will reach it, well, in my dreams.

Miss Julie Here we are chatting about dreams. Come. Let's go. Just into the park.

She offers her arm and they go.

Jean If we sleep on nine midsummer flowers tonight, our dreams will come true, Miss Julie.

*They turn to go. **Jean** holds his hand over one eye.*

Miss Julie What have you got in your eye?

Jean Oh, it's nothing. Only a bit of dirt, it'll be gone in a minute.

Miss Julie My sleeve must have brushed against you: sit down. Let me help you.

She takes him by the arm and sits him down. She takes hold of his head and leans it backwards; with the corner of her handkerchief she tries to remove the piece of dirt.

Miss Julie Sit still now; quite still. [*She slaps his hand.*] There, listen to me. [*Pause.*] I really believe he's trembling, the big strong boy. [*Feels his upper arm.*] With arms like that.

Jean Miss Julie!

__Christine__ has woken up, she goes, drowsy with sleep, to the right to lie down.

Miss Julie Yes, Monsieur Jean.

Jean Attention. Je ne suis qu'un homme!

Miss Julie Will you sit still? There! Gone! Now kiss my hand and thank me.

Jean Miss Julie. Listen to me. Christine has gone to bed, now will you listen to me.

Miss Julie Kiss my hand first.

Jean Listen to me.

Miss Julie Kiss my hand first.

Jean All right, but you'll only have yourself to blame.

Miss Julie For what?

Jean For what? You are not a child any more, you're 25. Don't you know it's dangerous to play with fire?

Miss Julie Not for me, I'm insured.

Jean [*boldly*] No, you're not. And even if you were there are other people who might catch fire.

Miss Julie Meaning you?

Jean Yes, but not just because it's me but because I am a man and young.

Miss Julie And handsome. You're so conceited. I suppose you think you're irresistible, don't you? Well I think you're all talk. I think you haven't got it in you.

Jean Do you think so?

Miss Julie I suspect so.

> **Jean** *moves forward intending to seize her round the waist and kiss her.* **Miss Julie** *slaps his face.*

Miss Julie Stop it.

Jean Are you serious or are you joking?

Miss Julie Serious!

Jean Then you were serious a moment ago as well! You play too seriously; it's dangerous. I'm tired of playing. If you'll excuse me I'll get back to my work. The Count's boots have to be polished and it's gone midnight.

Miss Julie Put the boots away!

Jean No, it's part of my job and I respect it. It's not my job to be your playmate though, and I never will be. I have too much self-respect.

Miss Julie Too much pride.

Jean In some ways, in others not.

Miss Julie Have you ever been in love?

Jean We don't use that expression, but I have loved. Once I fell ill because I couldn't get the girl I wanted. Like the princes in the 'Arabian Nights' who were so lovesick they couldn't eat or drink.

Miss Julie Who was she?

Jean doesn't reply.

Who was she?

Jean You can't force me to tell you that.

Miss Julie But if I ask you as an equal as a – friend! Who was she?

Jean It was you!

Context of the play

The critical response to August Strindberg's naturalistic tragedy in 1888 was hostile. The critics were as negative about Strindberg's preface as they were outraged by the content of the script. Why would a playwright wish to focus on such an unfortunate sequence of events exploring the doomed, brief relationship between a member of the serving classes and his master's troubled daughter? What audience in their right mind would want to see such events played out in such intimate detail?

Strindberg's preface outlines his intentions and beliefs about many of the controversial aspects of his play; his approach to character and characterization and his outspoken attitudes towards women and their relationships with men are as significant as his ideas about the role of theatre, class, monologue, plot, set and setting. Today the play is regarded as a classic and ground-breaking in its use of realism, yet is still seen by many as 'difficult' or challenging, especially in its portrayal of women and the contradictory, manipulative liaison between Jean and Miss Julie.

Significantly, the action of the play takes place over the course of a Midsummer Eve in the below-stairs kitchen of the Count's country manor. Unusually, Miss Julie has opted to stay and celebrate the evening with the servants rather than joining her father, visiting friends and relations of a more appropriate social standing. Miss Julie's enthusiastic dancing and unconventional behaviour have already surprised Jean, the Count's valet, and Christine, the cook.

Introductory task

1.   In a group of three or four, discuss the word *class*. What does this word mean when used to describe someone's place in society? What different types of class can your group name? Do you think that class is still important today?

2.   Read Jean's first few lines. Create a short improvisation that shows a group of servants and local villagers, standing at the edge of the dance floor and sneering at Miss Julie as she dances at the party. What sort of things might they say about her? Does anyone defend Miss Julie? Remember that the play was written over 100 years ago.

Task 1

1. In the extract, there are interesting and significant changes in status between all three characters. Who do you assume should have the highest status? Read the opening of the extract. When does Miss Julie lose the highest status? Working in your small group, choose a section of the text that you think shows the status shifting between the characters. Place a block or table and a few chairs in the performance space. Act out your chosen section, passing an object like a ball between the characters to symbolize the one who has dominant status.

2. Put the object away and rehearse your drama showing the status shifts through the way you say the dialogue, you body language and facial expression, and the way you place your body in relation to the other characters and the set.

Task 2

Much of what is said by the characters contains another level of meaning – they might say one thing, but mean something completely different. Sometimes there is significant meaning in silences and pauses. This is called sub-text. In your group, identify a few moments that you think have a noteworthy sub-text. Choose a section to explore. Using the script, rehearse the text, inserting lines of sub-text that express what you think the character is really saying. These could be said either by the actor playing the character or by another actor 'voicing' the lines.

Task 3

Symbols are very important in *Miss Julie*. Strindberg uses objects as symbols – such as the ever-present Count's boots – and also his characters talk about their hopes and dreams using symbols. Read the two long speeches in which Jean and Miss Julie talk about their dreams.

In your small group, represent both characters' dreams using abstract, stylized drama. Start by using either a still image or a series of repeated gestures to symbolize balancing, falling or climbing. Try to capture the movement quality experienced in dreams. Re-read the speeches and select some key lines that can be integrated into the drama. Experiment with different vocal qualities and techniques – whisper, echo, chant, staccato, unison, cannon.

Cultural references

1. Make a list of films, books, plays or stories where the main female character is portrayed as weak, evil or manipulative. Contrast this with films or plays that have strong and positive representations of women or where the woman is the hero. Which is the longer list?

2. Compare the play *Miss Julie* to a sub-plot in a modern television soap opera. Would it be effective in a modern setting?

Writing task

1. At the end of the extract Jean confesses he fell in love with an unobtainable girl, Miss Julie. Write a monologue in which Jean tells Miss Julie of the time he first saw her and fell in love. Remember they come from very different backgrounds. You might also want to consider whether Jean is telling the truth or making up a story that he thinks Miss Julie would like to hear.

2. Consider why Miss Julie did not go with her father to celebrate Midsummer Eve with their 'folk', but instead stayed at home with the servants. Write a short script featuring the Count and Miss Julie exploring this idea. Was the Count angry with Miss Julie for not accompanying him, or was she not allowed to come? Does it have anything to do with Miss Julie's recent engagement being broken off?

Hobson's Choice

Tanika Gupta

Characters in this extract

Hobson	owner of a successful dress-making business
Durga	
Ruby	Hobson's daughters
Sunita	
Ali Mossop	Hobson's best tailor
Pinky Khan	Ali's fiancée

Plot summary

Hari Hobson owns a tailor's shop in Salford. His three daughters – of whom the eldest, Durga, is the most headstrong – work in the shop for their father. Hobson insists that he will arrange marriages for the two youngest, but that Durga is 'past her sell by date'. However, Durga has other plans and decides to marry Hobson's best tailor, Ali Mossop. When Durga and Ali leave to set up business on their own, Hobson turns to drink. Tricked into giving presents of money to his youngest daughters as they marry, Hobson's condition worsens and he is forced to reconsider his position.

In this extract, Durga makes her catch.

Durga lifts the trap door and calls out.

Durga   Ali. Come here.

Ali Mossop appears and stops half-way up the trap.

Ali   Memsahib?

Durga   Come up and put the trap down. I need a word with you.

Ali comes up – reluctantly.

Ali   We're very busy in the basement.

Durga points to the trap.

He closes it.

Durga   Show me your hands.

Ali holds his hands out hesitatingly.

Clever hands. They can shape cloth like no other man that ever came into the business. Who taught you Ali?

She retains his hands.

Ali   My uncle – in Kolkatta. He was a tailor.

Durga   I didn't think it were me Baba. He doesn't know how to sew and cut. You're a natural at making clothes. It's a pity you're a natural fool as well.

Ali   I'm not much good at anything but sewing and that's a fact.

Durga   When are you going to leave here?

Ali   Leave here?

Durga   Don't you want to go?

Ali   Yes but … I've been at Hobson's since I first came to this country.

Durga   Don't you want to get on? You heard what Doctor Bannerji said. You know the wages you get and you know the wages a tailor like you could get in one of the exclusive shops in Manchester. Artisans like you are a dying breed.

Ali	I couldn't go.
Durga	What keeps you here? Is it the — the people?
Ali	Your Baba. He's the one that got me the work permit.
Durga	I see.
Ali	And he's got my passport.
Durga	And threatened to report you to the immigration authorities if you leave here?

Ali remains silent.

Do you know what keeps this business going? Two things: one's good cut clothes you make that sell themselves, the other's bad clothes the big manufacturers make and I sell. We're a pair, Ali Mossop.

Ali	You're a wonder in the shop Memsahib.
Durga	And you're a wizard in the workshop. So?
Ali	So ... what?
Durga	It's obvious.
Ali	What is?
Durga	You're leaving me to do all the work.
Ali	I'd better get back to my work.

Ali moves towards the trap.

Durga	[*Stopping him.*] I haven't finished with you. I've watched you for a long time and everything I've seen, I like. I think you'll do for me.

Ali looks anxious.

You're my man. I've been turning it over in my head for six months now. It's time for some action.

Ali	But I never —

Durga   I know you never, or it wouldn't be left to me to do the asking. And please –
stop calling me Memsahib. We're equals. My name is Durga.

Ali sits down in an armchair.

Ali   What d'you want me for?

Durga   To invest in. You're a business idea in the shape of a man.

Ali   I've got no head for business at all.

Durga   But I have. My brain and your hands'll make a working partnership.

Ali gets up relieved.

Ali   Partnership! Oh that's a different thing. I thought you were axing me to
marry you.

Durga   I am.

Ali   Heh – Allah! And you the Sahib's daughter.

Durga   Maybe that's why Ali. Maybe I've had enough of Baba and you're as different
from him as any man I know.

Ali   It's a bit difficult.

Durga   What's difficult? We get married and as my husband you can stay here –
permanently.

Ali   But …

Durga   I'll tell you something Ali. I'd be a fool to stand by and let the best chance of
my life slip through me fingers.

Ali   I'm your best chance?

Durga   You are that.

Ali   Heh Allah! I never thought of that.

Durga   Think of it now.

Ali   I am. But it's a bit of a shock … I can't think clear. I have much respect for
you Memsahib Durga. You're brilliant at selling in the shop and you've got a

shapely body but when it comes to marrying, well ... I'm sorry but I'm not in love with you.

Durga   Wait till you're asked. I want your hand in mine and your word that you'll go through life with me through thick and thin.

Ali   We won't get far without love.

Durga   I've got the love alright.

Ali   You're very determined on this. What would your Baba say? And me a Musulman?

Durga   He'll say a lot and he can say it. It'll make no difference to me.

Ali   Much better not to upset him. It's not worth it.

Durga   Let me be the judge of that. You're going to marry me Ali.

Ali   I can't do that. I can see that I'm messing up your plans ...

Durga   When I make plans, I follow them through.

Ali   What makes it so difficult is that ... I'm engaged.

Durga   You're what?

Ali   Pinky Khan.

Durga   Whose Pinky Khan?

Ali   I'm the lodger at her mother's.

Durga   That dark skinned slag who brings your lunch?

Ali   Pinky's fair skinned. And she'll be here soon.

Durga   And so shall I. I'll talk to Pinky. I've seen her and I know the type. She's the simpering, girly type.

Ali   She needs protecting.

Durga   That's how she got you is it? Yes, I can see her clinging round your neck until you imagined you were Sharukh Khan. But I can tell you this, my lad, she must be bloody desperate looking for protection from you.

Ali   Pinky loves me.

Durga   You marry her and you'll be broke all your life – slaving away for peanuts, trying to feed and clothe a tatty bunch of snot-nosed kids. You'll be a tailor on the minimum wage all your life exploited by Pinky on the one hand and the likes of my Baba on the other. Marry me and you'll be running your own business before long.

Ali   I'm not ambitious – I know that.

Durga   No, but you're going to be. Oh God, have I got my work cut out ...

Ali   I wish you'd leave me alone.

Durga   So does the fly when the spider catches him. You're my man, Ali Mossop.

Ali   But ... Pinky ...

Pinky Khan enters the shop. She is a meek-looking Asian girl dressed traditionally in synthetic fabrics. She brings in Ali's lunch in a tiffin carrier. Pinky crosses to Ali and gives him his lunch.

Pinky   [*Salford accent.*] There's your lunch Ali.

Ali   Thank you Pinky.

She turns to go and finds Durga in her way.

Durga   I want a word with you. You're treading on my foot.

Pinky looks stupidly at Durga's foot.

Pinky   Me?

Durga   What's this about you and him?

Pinky   [*Gushing.*] Oh Miss 'Obson, it's good of you to take an interest in us.

Ali   Pinky, she ...

Durga   Shush you. This is for me and her to sort out. Take a good look at him Pinky.

Pinky   At Ali?

Durga   [*Nodding.*] Not much for two women to have a scrap about is there?

Pinky   Maybe he's not much to look at, but you should hear him play.

Durga   Are you a musician Ali?

Ali   I play the ektara*

Durga   That's what you see in him is it? A gawky chap that plays the ektara?

Pinky   I see the man I love.

Durga   So do I.

Pinky   You!

Ali   That's what I've been trying to tell you, Pinky, and if you're not careful, she'll take me from you.

Pinky   Excuse me. You're too late. Me and Ali are engaged.

Durga   That's what you think.

Pinky   And I think you should mind your own business. Ali Mossop's mine.

Ali   That's what I tried to tell her but she won't listen.

Durga   How d'you plan to make a living together? If it's a better plan than mine, I'll wish you luck and you can have your man.

Pinky   He'll work and I'll keep house. Maybe I'll get meself a part time job but when we have kids, I'll stay at home. I want to be around then they're growing up.

Durga   It's worse than I thought. Ali, you better marry me.

Pinky   [*Weakly.*] It's daylight robbery.

Ali   Aren't you going to up a better fight for me than that Pinky?

Durga   You take orders from me in this shop.

Ali   Looks like there's no escape.

Pinky   Wait 'till I get you home. Ammi'll* have a few words to say to you.

Durga   Ah – so it's the tart's mother who set this up?

* One stringed instrument. Makes a twanging sound. Particularly used in Bangladesh folk singing.
*Muslim term for 'Mummy'.

Pinky	She called me a tart!
Ali	Her mother is keen on me.
Durga	Why don't you marry her then?
Ali	Don't be ridiculous.
Durga	I haven't got a mother Ali.
Ali	You don't need one.
Durga	Can I sell you a handkerchief, Miss Khan?
Pinky	No.
Durga	Then you've no business here have you?

Durga opens the door to the shop.

Pinky	Ali?
Durga	Goodbye.
Pinky	Are you going to let her order me out?
Ali	It's her shop Pinky.
Pinky	Is that it?
Ali	Best to go before things get violent.
Pinky	I'll show her violent …

Ali stands between the two women.

Ali	Pinky – please …
Pinky	It's a very shabby way to treat me.
Durga	When it comes to leaving, it's best to go quickly. No whimpering.
Pinky	I in't whimpering and I in't parting either. But he'll be bawling tonight when my Ammi gets hold of him.
Durga	That'll do.

Pinky exits.

Ali	I'd really rather marry Pinky, if it's all the same to you.
Durga	Why? Because of her 'Ammi'?
Ali	She's scary.
Durga	You wimp.
Ali	Yes, but you don't know her. She'll shout at me when I go home tonight. Very rough woman – who knows what else she'll do.
Durga	Then you won't go home tonight.
Ali	Not go!
Durga	Give up your room there. When you've knocked off work tonight you'll go to Tubby bhai's and Tubby'll go round to Pinky's for your things.
Ali	And I don't have to go back there ever?
Durga	No.

Ali smiles.

Durga	And while Tubby bhai's there you can go round and see Registrar about our wedding.
Ali	Oh, but I haven't got used to that idea yet.
Durga	You'll have three weeks to get used to it. A simple registry office affair – that way we don't have to worry about Priests or Mullahs. Now, kiss me Ali.
Ali	That's forcing things a bit. It's like saying I agree to everything, a kiss is.
Durga	Yes.
Ali	And I don't agree yet, I'm –
Durga	Come on.

Ruby and Sunita enter from the house.

Get on with it.

Ali   Now? With them here?

Durga   Yes.

Beat.

Ali   I couldn't.

Ali ducks back down through the trap door and slams the door shut behind him.

Sunita   What's the matter with Ali?

Durga   He's a bit upset because I've told him he's going to marry me. How's lunch getting on?

Ruby   Hold up, what did you say?

Durga   You heard me.

Sunita   You're going to marry Ali Mossop? Ali Mossop?

Ruby   You kept that quiet.

Durga   I've only just proposed.

Ruby   How could you?!

Sunita   What you do effects us. I don't want Ali Mossop for my brother-in-law.

Durga   Why? What's wrong with him?

Sunita   Let's see what Baba has to say. And what about me? What about Steve?

Durga   You'll marry Steve when he's able and that'll be when he starts spending less on clothes and season tickets to watch Man U.

Hobson enters from the street.

Hobson   Where's my lunch?

Durga   It'll be ready in ten minutes.

Hobson   You said one o'clock.

Durga   One for half-past. If you wash your hands it'll be ready as soon as you are.

Ruby   Have you heard the news about our Durga?

Hobson News? There is no news. It's the same old tale. Cheek, arrogance and disrespect.

Durga Don't lose your temper. You'll need to be calm when Ruby tells you the news.

Hobson What's Ruby been doing?

Ruby Nothing. It's about Ali Mossop.

Hobson Ali?

Sunita What's your opinion of him?

Hobson A decent boy. I've got nothing against him.

Sunita Would you like him in the family?

Hobson Whose family?

Ruby Yours.

Durga I'm going to marry Ali Mossop. That's what all the fuss is about.

Hobson What?!

Durga You thought I was past the marrying age. I'm not. That's it. That's the news.

Hobson Didn't you hear me say I'd do the choosing when it came to the question of husbands?

Durga You said I was too old to get a husband.

Hobson You are. You all are.

Ruby Baba!

Hobson And if you're not, it makes no difference. I'll have no husbands here.

Sunita But you said –

Hosbson I've changed my mind. I've learnt some things since then. Too much is expected of fathers these days. There'll be no weddings here.

Sunita Oh Baba!

Hobson Shut up and get my lunch served. Go on now. I'm not in the mood to hear your rantings.

Hobson *shoos* **Sunita** *and* **Ruby** *away. They exit protesting loudly.*

But **Durga** *stands in his way as he follows and she closes the door.*

Durga	I'm not a fool and neither are you. Let's talk straight and get this sorted.
Hobson	You can't have Ali Moissop. For a start he's a Muslim, secondly he's half-cast and thirdly – his father was a hippy – and Ali's a come-by-chance …
Durga	Eh?

Hobson *covers* **Lord Ganesha's** *ears.*

Hobson	… A bastard. His father shacked up with his mother and legged it when Ali was born.
Durga	Makes no difference to me. I'll have Ali Mossop. I've decided what I want so you'd better get used to it.
Hobson	If I allowed it – I'd be the laughing stock of the Asian Small Businesses Association of Salford. I won't have it Durga.

Hobson *moves across to the statue of* **Ganesha,** *touches his belly and does pranam.**

It's indecent at your time of life.

Durga	I'm thirty and I'm marrying Ali. And now I'll mek a deal with you.
Hobson	You're hardly in a position to make deals.
Durga	You will pay Ali the same wages as before. I've worked for sixteen years for you, free of charge. I'll do eight hours a day in future and you will pay me £300 per week.
Hobson	D'you think I'm made of money?
Durga	You'll be made of less money if you let Ali go. And if Ali goes, I go. Face facts.
Hobson	I could face it Durga. Shop hands are cheap.

*Paying respect. An action where the person usually touches the feet of an elder in blessing.

Durga	Cheap ones are cheap. The type you'd have to watch all day to make sure they're not fiddling the books or robbing the till. Maybe you don't mind Jim, Rohan and Sanjay having a drink without you. I'm worth it and so's Ali. Imagine, you can show off at The Nelson that you married me off to a decent, hard working man. If I were you, I'd put my hand in my pocket and do what I propose.
Hobson	I'll show you what I propose.

Hobson calls.

Ali Mossop!

Hobson unbuckles his belt and places his hat on the counter.

I can't beat you. I never raised a hand to you but I can beat him. Come up Ali Mossop.

Ali enters.

Hobson conceals the belt.

You've taken a shine to my Durga I hear.

Ali	No, not me. It was her.
Hobson	Well, Ali, either way, you've fallen on misfortune. Love's led you astray and I have to put you straight.

Hobson shows the belt.

Ali	Durga, what's this?
Durga	I'm watching you, my lad.
Hobson	You can keep your job. I don't hold grudges but we must beat the love from your body and every morning you come here to work with love still sitting in you, you'll get a beating.

Hobson gets ready to strike.

Ali	You can't beat love into me. You're making a great mistake Sahib, and …
Hobson	You'll waste a lot of money at chemist's if I'm at you for a week with this.

Hobson *swings the belt.*

Ali I don't want your Durga, it's her that's after me but I'll tell you this Sahib – if you touch me with that belt, I'll take her quick, yes and stick to her like glue.

Hobson There's only one answer to that kind of talk, beta*.

Hobson *strikes* **Ali** *with the belt.*

Durga *shrinks.*

Ali And I've only one answer back. Durga, I didn't kiss you before. Allah be merciful, I'll kiss you now.

Ali *kisses* **Durga** *quickly, with temper, not with passion, and as quickly turns to face* **Hobson**.

And I'll take you and hold you. And if the Sahib raises that belt again, I'll do more. I'll walk straight out of shop with you and we two will set up for ourselves.

Durga Hey – Ali. I knew you had it in you!

Hobson *stands in amazed indecision.*

* Lad

Context of the play

This play is a new version of Harold Brighouse's 1916 comedy set in Salford, which tells the story of the domineering Henry Horatio Hobson, and how he is finally defeated by his long-suffering daughters. Tanika Gupta updated and transposed the play, originally set in a cobbler's shop, to a contemporary British Asian setting. In Gupta's version, 'Hari' Hobson and his daughters, Sunita, Ruby and the feisty Durga, run a tailoring business.

In this extract, Durga begins to hatch her plot to marry the oppressed but skilful tailor Ali Mossop, and take over the family business. Her father, however, has other ideas.

Introductory task

Create still images based on the following lines of dialogue:

I'm not much good at anything but sewing and that's a fact. (p.41)

My brain and your hands'll make a working partnership. (p.43)

Aren't you going to put up a better fight for me than that, Pinky? (p.46)

I'm thirty and I'm marrying Ali. And now I'll mek a deal with you. (p.51)

There's only one answer to that kind of talk, beta. (p.53)

Consult the text, and try to show the relationship between the various characters at those moments in the play.

Task 1

1.   Stage the scene from the entry of Pinky Khan until she exits. What does this episode tell us about the character of Durga? What advice would you give to the actor playing Durga?

2.   Rehearse the section, taking note of the way that the status of the three characters shifts from one to the other. As you rehearse, pause at key moments to identify who has the status – perhaps by awarding marks out of 10.

3.   How does this exercise help you to understand this section of the scene?

Task 2

1.   At one point Hobson remarks that if he allows the marriage between Ali and Durga to go ahead, he will 'be the laughing stock of the Asian Small Businesses Association of Salford'. Why do you think Hobson says this?

2.   Imagine that news of the marriage has become public. Improvise a scene that takes place at the next meeting of the association. Begin the scene as Hobson arrives at the meeting: *Now then Hari, what's this we hear…?*

Cultural references

In her introduction to the play, Tanika Gupta writes that 'sweatshop labourers are not only found in Indonesia and Malaysia but here in the UK too'. What does she mean by 'sweatshop labour'?

Find out where your favourite items of clothing were manufactured. Many High Street fashions are produced by workers who receive very low wages for their work. How much more would you be prepared to pay so that they could receive better wages? What could be done to help these workers?

Writing task

1.   Compare this extract with the extract from Ayub Khan-Din's play *East is East*, also found in this collection. In many ways the plays are similar. Write down as many ways in which they differ as you can.

2.   Concentrate on the way that dialogue is handled between the members of the families in the two plays. Which do you think is more 'realistic', and why? Give examples of dialogue from both plays to illustrate your ideas.

The Colour of Justice

Richard Norton-Taylor

Characters in this extract

Lawson	Edmund Lawson, QC, Counsel to the Inquiry
Groves	Inspector Steven Groves, in charge of scene-of-the-crime operations on the night of the murder
Mansfield	Michael Mansfield, QC, the Lawrence family's lawyer
Macdonald	Ian Macdonald, QC, leading counsel for Stephen Lawrence's best friend, Duwayne Brooks
Macpherson	a retired High Court judge, Chairman of the Stephen Lawrence Inquiry

Plot summary

Stephen Lawrence, a young black man, was the victim of a racist attack on Thursday 22nd April, 1993. He was stabbed to death in South London.

The Colour of Justice is made up entirely of extracts from the Macpherson inquiry into the incident and is a damning indictment of British society's racism. In the dramatisation, evidence and eyewitnesses point to five white youths as responsible for the crime, yet five years later no one has been brought to justice.

In this extract, we witness a scene in which Inspector Groves give evidence.

**From the Evidence of Inspector
Groves, 1 and 2 April 1998**

Lawson   You're an inspector serving in the Metropolitan Police?

Groves   Yes, that's right.

Lawson   Currently serving where?

Groves   Westminster.

Lawson   Mr Groves, already on the screen is a copy of the statement made by you in May 1993. The matters you were being asked particularly to address, page 24 of volume 50, it is right there: questions of consideration being given to neglect of duty in respect of failure to ensure a record was kept at the scene and a failure in respect of first-aid treatment?

Groves   That's right, sir.

Lawson   Moving back to PCA 38, page 303, may I ask you this – this is obviously dealing with the events of the evening of the 22nd of April 1993 – I understand, is this correct, that you have no surviving notes?

Groves   No, sir, I have not.

Lawson   There was reference to you having a clipboard at the scene?

Groves   I still have the clipboard. I don't have any notes.

Lawson   What happened to them, do you know?

Groves   The notes I made that night were fairly comprehensive. They were taken by me at their request to Shooter's Hill Police Station a little while later.

Lawson   Are you able to give an indication of what time you got to the scene?

Groves   No, not really. I would think about 10.45.

Lawson   Would you regard yourself as having been in charge of the scene?

Groves   Yes.

Lawson   Had you been given an inkling as to what had happened to Stephen Lawrence, apart from the fact that you had been told he had been assaulted with an iron bar and had serious head injuries?

Groves   No sir.

Lawson   Had you asked anybody at the scene if they could assist with what had happened?

Groves   Yes.

Lawson   What were you told?

Groves   I did not have any information.

Lawson   The very distraught young man who was there was Duwayne Brooks – WPC Bethel managed to calm him down sufficiently to get some account from him about what happened, but that was never passed to you?

Groves   No, sir, I don't think so. I carried on walking to the pub.

Lawson   You learned nothing from that?

Groves   No, nothing at all.

Lawson   Your account is that a variety of streets in the neighbourhood were directed by you to be searched by police, some with dogs, is that right?

Groves   The one that happened at midnight, the main search, the very, very, thorough search.

Lawson   Nothing, in fact, was found, was it?

Groves   I have a feeling that the only thing one of them found was – I do not think it was anything to do with this. I think it was a salt pot.

Lawson   Was a report made to you that night about the red Astra. Does that mean anything to you?

Groves   No, sir. I don't think so. I don't recall.

Lawson   Thank you.

Mansfield   So everybody knows exactly what it is that is being suggested on behalf of Mr and Mrs Lawrence in relation to you, I just want to pick out some of those.

First of all, it is suggested that you failed to take proper control of the scene upon arrival as the first senior officer.

Secondly, you failed to discover relevant information in order to exercise proper control.

Thirdly, you failed to order and monitor an effective and immediate search for offenders by means of mobile, house-to-house and witness search.

Fourthly, the failure of one to three arose because of your assumptions about the nature of the offence and the victim – race.

The first question I want to ask you, officer, is looking back on it all now, is there anything you think first of all that went wrong as the senior officer between 11 and 1.30 in the morning with the investigation under you?

Groves   No, sir, I don't think so.

Mansfield   Nothing?

Groves   With the investigation, no.

Mansfield   Right. I am going to suggest to you that there was a great deal more that you could have done which might have resulted in something, it might not, do you follow?

Groves   Yes, sir, certainly.

Mansfield   To use your own words to the Kent investigation: 'Unless you search an area thoroughly and quickly, then you are losing evidence all of the time'?

Groves   That's right, sir.

Mansfield   And I suggest to you that you were losing evidence every minute that went by that night, were you not?

Groves   I would absolutely agree with you.

Mansfield   Right. So where did it go wrong, officer?

Groves   Where did what go wrong?

Mansfield   Let us start with a fairly basic matter. Which carrier were you on when you went to the scene?

Groves   I am not sure. The carrier that had Clement on it, 325 I believe.

Mansfield Clement was in charge of 325, was he?

Groves Yes.

Mansfield Clement was in charge of 326.

Groves Was he?

Mansfield Was he? Well, do not ask me. I am asking you. Before we get going on this, Mr Groves, I am going to suggest this inquiry cannot rely on a single word you are saying. Do you think you are totally unreliable?

Groves No, sir.

Mansfield I want to ask you very carefully about those notes. When did you last see them?

Groves In 1993.

Mansfield What did you do with them?

Groves I took them to Shooters Hill.

Mansfield When?

Groves A little while later.

Mansfield When? The same day? The next day? Within a week?

Groves I am not sure.

Mansfield I would like you to think.

Groves Well, I have thought about it for five years.

Mansfield I am sure you have.

Groves You will get the same answer: I am not sure.

Mansfield I suggest there is a very strong possibility that there were never any notes. Do you follow, Mr Groves?

Groves Yes, I do.

Mansfield How many sheets were involved, roughly speaking?

Groves   I don't know, sir. I could not answer that.

Mansfield   And the notes have never come to light, have they?

Groves   No, they haven't.

Mansfield   No one has seen these notes with diagrams, dustbins and all the rest of it, no one but you?

Groves   It would certainly make both of our lives very much easier had I got my notes.

Mansfield   You talk about photocopying. Now what happened to the photocopies?

Groves   I keep copies of most documents I think I might need. I certainly think I would have kept copies of this.

Mansfield   So where are they?

Groves   This is five years ago. I have not got my copies any more. I have not got them. It would help not only me but it would help the inquiry if I could find the copies. I have not got them. I cannot say more than that. I have not got them.

Mansfield   Have you destroyed them?

Groves   Very probably, yes.

Mansfield   Well, did you, and if so when, and why did you not tell Kent: 'I destroyed them'?

Groves   I cannot recall destroying them.

Mansfield   Why would you destroy them?

Groves   I had no reason to keep them past three years.

Mansfield   This case you knew was trundling on in one way or another? You knew that from the publicity?

Groves   Yes, of course.

Mansfield   Is there any possibility, officer, that you just never took any notes that night because you were not that bothered about this incident? Is that a possibility?

Groves   No. When somebody dies it is something that I remember for the rest of my life. I don't just – whether they are black or white is irrelevant, if that is what you are getting at.

Mansfield When you went to the scene, Mr Groves, you did not treat this as a murder enquiry, did you?

Groves I think I certainly did …

Mansfield I want you to think very carefully. The question is, when you first went to the scene, you did not treat this as a murder enquiry, did you?

Groves Well, not when Stephen was alive.

Mansfield He was dead, I suggest, when you got there?

Groves I don't think he was. When I knew Stephen had died this was something very, very different. It was now a murder enquiry.

Mansfield Let us get utterly clear what you thought about this when you first got to the scene. What did you think about it?

Groves I thought that what we were dealing with here was possibly a fight.

Mansfield A fight?

Groves Sir, if you keep interrupting me, I shall just slow down. It is important that I am allowed to give my answers here and it is not easy with you interrupting. When I arrived at the scene, I was an unconscious person and my concern was who had done that to that person and I had to think about what I was going to do about finding the person or persons responsible.

Mansfield I am waiting because I did not …

Groves I have finished. Please …

Mansfield Now, may I use these words, which I suggest are your words. When you first got to the scene, it was just an assault and that is all.

Groves It was a serious assault. We had to act on the information that we had.

Mansfield I am going to put to you, Mr Groves, that I suggest to you very clearly this is one of your assumptions because it is a black victim, was it not?

Groves   No, sir. You are accusing me of being a racist now and that is not true. I would like it noted that I do not think that is fair either. You have no evidence that I am racist.

Mansfield   If I ask you if you are a racist what will you say?

Groves   Of course I am not. I could not do my job if I was a racist, it would not be possible, it is not compatible.

Mansfield   You agree you describe the assault as a fight and you say that was based on information?

Groves   I think what I said was that is what I thought I was dealing with, an assault, a fight. That is right.

Mansfield   I am going to ask you carefully. I am going to suggest this is where the approach or attitude of mind to race is important. You did say before that was the message, that it was a fight. Is that right you had information or was that an assumption by you?

Groves   I have now said that five times. I have said five times that the information that I had was this was a fight. Do you want me to say it six times for you, would that make it clearer for you? I am not going to elaborate on this.

Mansfield   I suggest to you, Mr Groves, I am going to interrupt, there was no information being fed to the police that this man suffered an injury as the result of a fight?

Groves   In that case you are wrong.

Mansfield   Where did you say it came from?

Groves   I think the call we got, the original call was possibly from the information room.

Mansfield   You see, the information that the inquiry has been told was effectively, an assault with an iron bar, quite different to a fight. In other words, somebody being attacked. This was your information, Mr Groves?

Groves   Sir, of course, I would agree with you.

Mansfield   You translated, I suggest to you, the information of an assault into: black man on pavement involved in fight. Is that a possibility?

Groves   Of course that is a possibility, absolutely. Absolutely.

Mansfield   Yes.

Groves   It is not an assumption, it is a possibility.

Mansfield   If you saw a police officer on the ground with injuries and you had been told about an assault with an iron bar, would you assume a fight?

Groves   I would have to consider it, of course.

Mansfield   Moving forward, you were asked specifically questions about the race issue, were you not, by Kent?

Groves   Yes.

Mansfield   What is the word that you use most regularly to describe non-white people?

Groves   Black people.

Mansfield   Do you?

Groves   Coloured people.

Mansfield   Coloured people is the word you most commonly use, is it not?

Groves   Okay. I am in a sort of quandary here. He is a white man, that is a coloured woman. [*Indicating.*] What else can I say. I have to make some description. I do not think that is being racist. He is a white man, he is a white man, that is a coloured man. [*Indicating.*]

Mansfield   I am going to bring it back to the scene, as it were. Did the thought that night, since you kept your options open, ever come across your mind this was a racist attack?

Groves   Not initially, no.

Mansfield   No.

Groves   Not until I had enough information to make, using your word, an 'assumption'.

Mansfield   Yes, thank you.

Macdonald   Were you aware that Duwayne Brooks had told WPC Bethel that as they were coming across the road to attack, they had shouted some racist abuse?

Groves   No, sir, I was not aware of that.

Macdonald   'What, what nigger.'

Groves   No sir.

Macdonald   You told us that you understood that the injuries that Stephen Lawrence had came from a fight?

Groves   No, that was the information we had.

Macdonald   Can I ask you this: is that why you went to the pub?

Groves   A pub is an absolute mine of information. You can learn more from pubs from people who have had a drink than knocking on doors at 11 o'clock.

Macpherson   Thank you very much, Mr Groves.

Context of the play

In April 1993, black teenager Stephen Lawrence was stabbed to death in a racist attack by a group of white youths. The police launched an investigation, but failed to gather enough evidence to convict Stephen's murderers. Amid much controversy a public enquiry was launched, which revealed serious defects in the way the investigation into Stephen's death was undertaken. The police force that conducted it was accused of 'institutionalized racism'.

The Colour of Justice is a 'documentary drama' based on the transcripts of the 69-day public enquiry. The play takes place in a single setting – a court room – and consists of nothing but the (heavily edited) words of those who conducted and gave evidence to the enquiry.

This extract is the evidence of one of the police officers in charge of the investigation into the murder, who was among the first to attend the scene of the crime.

Introductory task

1. What do you think is meant by the term 'documentary drama'? Are you familiar with any other plays (or films) in this form?

2. What is the effect of using the words actually spoken by the police officer? Why not change the words to make the scene more 'dramatic'? Try improvising a section of the scene using your own words. What is the effect?

3. One other play in this collection, Mark Wheeller's *Too Much Punch for Judy*, also makes use of the words spoken by real people, but in *Too Much Punch* this is interspersed with clearly 'fictional' passages. Read the extract from Wheeller's play. How does it compare?

4. Some people distrust the mixture of documentary (truth) and drama (fiction) in plays like these. Why do you think this is? What is your opinion?

Task 1

1. Stage the scene. In order to be most effective, how should the stage space be used? What staging set-up is best: end on, in-the-round or traverse, perhaps?

Why? Who might the audience 'represent' in this play? Which set-up best suggests this?

2. What set is necessary? How can the relationship between Sir William Macpherson, who chaired the enquiry, the lawyers and the police officer be represented by the way you choose to use the space?

3. Draw a sketch of the stage layout you chose for the scene.

Task 2

At first sight you may feel that not much happens in the scene!

1. As you perform the scene, try to identify the key moments – perhaps where tension is heightened or where emotion is revealed. See whether you can find moments where there is a clear sub-text – perhaps by pausing to speak the thoughts of the characters at particular moments in order to reveal contrasts with what is actually spoken. As you rehearse, try to include as much detail in your acting as possible in order to bring out these subtle changes in mood, relationship and dramatic tension.

2. How far should the police officer – who is clearly unsettled by the lawyer's questioning – lose his temper? What about the lawyers, particularly Mansfield? How do they relate to the policeman?

3. How should the final part of the scene be played for best effect?

Cultural references

What do you think is meant by the term 'institutionalized racism?' Why do you think the case of Stephen Lawrence has proved so controversial?

Writing task

In the scene, Inspector Groves reveals that his notes for the evening of 22 April – the night Stephen Lawrence was stabbed – have been mislaid. Based on your reading of the scene, compile a page of notes that might have been written by the officer, describing his actions on the night in question. Begin:

22 April 1993, 10.45pm: Arrived at scene of crime to find...

Too Much Punch for Judy

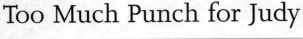

Mark Wheeller

Characters in this extract

Judy	the driver
Jo	Judy's sister
P.C. Caten	policeman called to accident, friend of Jo and Judy
P.C. Abrahams	police constable
Duncan	witness to accident

Plot summary

Sisters Jo and Judy follow up an aerobics session with a visit to the local wine bar, where they both have a drink. On the way home, on a lonely road in Essex, the car comes off the road and hits a bridge. The scaffolding construction slices through the car. The driver, Judy, escapes unhurt, but Jo is killed outright.

In this extract, local resident Duncan witnesses the accident.

Section 3: The Accident

Judy   We'd been to the Epping Sports Centre doing an aerobics class, and after a couple of drinks there we went on to the Wine bar. It was only around the corner so we walked. I wasn't drinking as much as Jo; I hadn't had an enormous amount; I should imagine about three quarters of a bottle of wine which to me isn't a lot of drink. I certainly didn't *feel* drunk. Jo had drunk an awful lot so I suggested that it would be better if I drove:

Jo   No! It's my car. It's my responsibility.

Judy   Jo, what's going to happen if you do get pulled up? You'll go to court with two drink drive convictions which means a huge ban and a ridiculous fine!

Jo   No, it's my car!

Judy   Look, I haven't had as much to drink as you, so I'm only going to be a bit over the limit and anyway, even if I did get caught, it makes no odds 'cos I don't need to drive as much as you what with your job and …

Jo   Ok then. You drive …

Jo throws the car keys to Judy. They freeze the moment as Judy catches the keys. Silence.

Judy   We got into the car with me in the driving seat and put a tape on.

WE'VE ONLY JUST BEGUN* by the Carpenters fades in slowly and underpins the duration of the accident scene.

It's only about five miles from the Epping Sports centre to North Weald where I live. The last thing I remember is driving past the hospital.

P.C. Caten   I was out with a fairly young PC. We'd been static at Scratch Bridge in North Weald for about half an hour.

P.C. Abrahams   As far as I can remember, it was about five to twelve and we'd decided to go in at midnight to have a cup of tea.

P.C. Caten   As we made our way towards Epping, I happened to note Jo and Judy drive by. I'd known their family for … well over ten years. I supposed they'd been out enjoying themselves.

*The performing rights for this play do not cover the right to use this or other pieces of pre-recorded music. Permission will be required from the appropriate bodies.

Judy   I was used to driving a bigger car with powered steering and I guess what must have happened is that where I was a bit drunk I forgot I was in Jo's car and just didn't turn the wheel enough on this bend at Scratch Bridge. I can't remember going off the road, I can't remember hitting the kerb or anything. God, it must have took off when we hit that kerb. Every now and then I get flashbacks, I keep thinking that she told me to slow down, but I can't remember her being in the car. I can't really remember anything.

Actor 1   Ok then; you drive

Actor 2   No it's my car it's my responsibility.

Actor 1   I think I'll make a will.

Actor 2   I'm only going to be a bit over the limit.

Actor 1   Them two. They're always pissed they'll be alright.

Actor 2   I got the death card both times.

Actor 1   Today's easy to follow recipe 'Smashed out of our Skulls'.

Actor 1 & 2   Ok then. You drive.

Jo   Judy! Slow down a bit!

Judy   Wouldn't it be better if I drove? What's going to happen if you do get pulled up? You'll go to court with two drink drive convictions which means a huge ban and a ridiculous fine!

I haven't had as much to drink as you, so I'm only going to be a bit over the limit and anyway, even if I did get caught, it makes no odds. I don't need to drive as much as you what with your job and …

The accident is simulated stylistically somehow!!! It has been presented in a variety of ways. I would suggest the use of scaffolding bars and loud screams … attempting to capture the essence of the accident … speed … impact … fright … whiplash … the sound of metal on metal … and finally silence and stillness.

Section 4: The Aftermath

Duncan   I guess it was about midnight and there was one hell of a mighty crash, completely and utterly unannounced by any of the normal sounds that one might associate with a road accident … howls of tyres, screeching and what have you.

I was just mesmerised. I couldn't think what it was and all I could hear was 'We've Only Just Begun' by the Carpenters blasting out from what I later discovered to be the car stereo. I got out of bed and looked out of the window.

Slide 1*

There was a Renault 5 buried in the bridge, just literally sort of disappeared into the bridge parapet. My immediate reaction was 'Oh shit! I don't want to be involved in that! I'll let someone else go and have a look.' I waited … maybe half a minute, hoping that someone would get out of the bloody thing … but nobody did. In the end, I pulled on a pair of trousers, a pullover but stupidly nothing else and shot across there.

I couldn't approach the car from the passenger side it was too badly damaged so went to the driver's door. It wouldn't open. I looked inside. I could see two shapes. I tried the door again. The music was blasting out, like it was sort of force ten on the decibel scale.

At that point I suddenly realised that I was standing around in bare feet with a lot of glass about the place which was pretty bloody stupid. I thought … 'well, nobody else is coming out to help!', so I shot back inside, dialled 999, reported the accident … oh yes … and put some shoes on!

P.C. Abrahams   We'd only gone about half a mile further, towards the police station, when our information room called up.

Voice   [FX *over radio.*] Any unit to attend a serious RTA in North Weald.

Slide 2

P.C. Abrahams   We can attend. We're in North Weald. Can you give us an exact location?

Voice   [FX *over radio.*] The informant is telephoning from Harrison Drive. The accident was on Scratch Bridge.

---

* Slides, police photos of the accident to be shown in this scene are available from MBA Literary Agents Limited, 62 Grafton Way, London W1P 5LD (Tel: 020 7387 2076 Fax: 020 7387 2042 E-mail: meg@mbalit.co.uk. They should be requested when seeking performing rights.

P.C. Abrahams   We'll attend. E.T.A. one minute.

Duncan   I went back to the car which was now smelling of petrol, battery fluid, anti-freeze and there was this dripping and hissing. I was afraid it might catch fire so, put my leg up onto the back wing and forced the driver's side door open.

The music was blasting out, so the first thing I did was to turn off the power which produced dead silence.

I was then confronted with these two forms and a strong smell of alcohol. I remember that clearly, the smell of alcohol and ... well, cheap perfume.

I felt for a pulse on the passenger. I couldn't find one. There was no ... no life signs at all. [*Pause.*]

Slide 3

The bridge they'd hit was just these upright concrete pillars with scaffolding pipes coming through them.

One of these pipes had been bent, come straight in, through the windscreen, missed the driver ... but it was such that the passenger had to have been hit by it. Her head was in a position where it had obviously been thrown back by the force of this pole coming in directly on ... to her face. I was sufficiently squeamish not to investigate that one any further. Thank Christ it wasn't bloody daylight, that's all I can say.

I remember thinking ... 'the passenger is either dead or alive. If she's dead, well I can't do anything about it, but what if she starts to wake up, with hideous bloody injuries requiring some attention, what the bloody hell am I to do then?'

I've done my bit of first aid, but this was way, way, way beyond that ... or anything I'd experienced in my life.

That's the frightening thing about it. The fact that she was dead ... was a bloody blessing!

He goes to **Judy**.

By this time the driver had begun to make signs of recovery, so I managed to find the buckles of her seat belt and release her.

'Right, let's get you out of here.'

She was like a sort of bendy toy really ... I soon realised that she was smashed out of her skull ... drunk.

Judy   What on earth happened down there?

Duncan   I'm afraid you've had a bit of an accident dear. Can you tell me what your name is?

Judy   Judy. [*Pause.*]

There was glass in the car. I remember glass and blood on the floor of the car; where did it all come from?

Duncan   We'll find out later.

Judy   Where's my handbag? I want my handbag! It must be in the car!

Duncan   No, you hang on here a minute love.

Judy   My sister! I've got to get to Joanna! She's still in the car! Don't you bloody touch me! I want to go and see if she's alright!

Duncan   No! We'd better wait here. I've phoned the police, so they'll be here in a minute.

Judy   What's wrong with Joanna? Fucking let go of me!

She crumples. Resigned.

Why won't you let me go back to the car?

Duncan   I thought she was going to get so hysterical that I just wouldn't be able to cope, but she didn't actually; she just seemed to go limpish and start to cry.

At that point the police car came down the road like a bat out of hell! I don't think that it had stopped before the doors were opened and a young PC ran out towards us.

There's someone else in the car.

P.C. Abrahams   I'll go down.

Duncan   He went down to the passenger side of the vehicle and shone a torch in there. Obviously he was having difficulty seeing inside because he kept angling his head.

P.C. Caten   It's Jo Poulton. I can't believe it! Jo and Judy.

P.C. Abrahams   Do you know them then?

P.C. Caten   Yeh. I can't get a pulse at all!

P.C. Abrahams   Look! Smoke under the bonnet.

P.C. Caten   You go and get the extinguisher … I'll phone HQ and then go and see the driver … she's Jo's sister.

> *Abrahams exits.* **P.C. Caten** *speaking to radio.*

Golf -golf -two -one. Regarding RTA that we are attending in North Weald. We require immediate back up. Possible fatal. We require two ambulances. I repeat two ambulances.

Duncan   I can remember holding this woman, listening to him report back and nodding as he said 'fatal'. She didn't hear anything. I'm absolutely positive that she had no idea at all … though she must have surely suspected something.

P.C. Caten   Thanks for your help. It's good of you to come out.

Duncan   Is it OK for me to go back home now?

P.C. Caten   Yeh. I know Judy … don't I love … so I'll make sure that she's OK. Thanks again for coming out.

Duncan   I live over there. If you want any further information … feel free to knock.

I went back home and poured myself a great big bloody drink! I opened the curtains and stood and watched the proceedings … just out of morbid curiosity … I'm afraid that's inherent in all of us in those kinds of circumstances. I remember feeling slightly angry that so many houses that faced onto it had obviously decided that they didn't want to become involved … it's just a silly sort of reaction you get in a state of stress … 'cos I do understand why ... but bloody muggings here ... why did I have to go out and get involved?

I didn't sleep at all. The realisation that you've come right next to an extremely violent death was a very unnerving and shattering experience ... and it was annoying. This bloody woman who drive this bloody car hadn't even touched the brakes ... well she couldn't have done! There wasn't a mark on the road anywhere! She was that drunk! She didn't even know that she'd gone up the kerb, along the pavement and into the bridge parapet ... she was that drunk!

P.C. Caten My main job now was to keep Judy away from the accident and her mind off Jo. She had glass in her hair, blood on her fingers, was very disoriented and continued to cry. I carried her to the police car and spoke to her to reassure her that everything that could be done was being done. Eventually the ambulance arrived.

'Judy, where's your daughter? Where's Leanne?'

Judy She's at home. I've got a baby-sitter. What'll happen?

P.C. Caten It's Ok. I'll sort something out whilst you're being taken to the hospital.

Judy What about Joanna? Isn't she coming?

P.C. Caten They're just getting her out. She'll be coming in another ambulance.

Judy Why can't she come in this one?

P.C. Caten I'm afraid that she's a bit more hurt than you are.

Judy Why can't we wait? I want her to come with me!

P.C. Caten No! We need another ambulance for her.

Judy I remember turning round as they put me in the ambulance and seeing the car hooked on the railings up in the air. I didn't see the front of the car at all. They kept me round my side of the car which was alright. It weren't smashed or nothing ... It was all up in the air and like tipping forward and the wheels were off the ground and I thought ... 'Oh look at that!!' I didn't think that Jo had been really injured ... it didn't even enter my mind that she could have been killed.

P.C. Abrahams After they'd got the passenger out of the car I had to keep members of the public who'd come out to watch away from the scene as it wasn't a particularly pretty sight. When they started to get her out of the car they realised that she had quite severe injuries so they had to … somebody got some black plastic bags which they put over her head and shoulders … just to make it a little better for people that were gathered around.

P.C. Caten We made our way to her mother's house. We had to break the news to her. I will admit that I was controlling my feelings more than I've ever had to before.
I took a deep breath and knocked on the door.

P.C. Abrahams There was no reply. We tried several times again.

P.C. Caten That's strange. Judy said she'd be in.

P.C. Abrahams No one answered so we came away.

As this speech is portrayed any 'debris' from the accident can be cleared up.

I've recently been reading THE SHOOTING OF PRESIDENT KENNEDY. He was apparently lying in the hospital after he died and the hospital was returning to normal. There was a comment made, that next door, two janitors … auxiliaries were laughing … laughing over a joke. There was this hollow laughter going down the corridor with a dead president there … a very harsh irony eh? Well, a similar thing happened in this situation. The ambulance had gone, and you were left with the 'roadies' trying to drag the car off the bridge parapet. They were laughing and I thought … that can't be right.

My final reaction was the following morning. I went out there and 'society' had cleared up the mess. 'Society' had come along with its back up force and cleaned up the mess … you know … the ambulance had taken away the broken body … and the mortuary had taken care of it from then on.

There wasn't any blood … there wasn't anything. The place had been sanitised.

It was an extraordinary sensation, and yet a human life had disappeared there, and you felt … well I felt that there should be something there that actually proved the point … but there was nothing.

Context of the play

Too Much Punch for Judy dramatizes the tragic events surrounding a real drink-driving accident. Two sisters, Joanna and Judy, are travelling home after a night out when the car they are in skids off the road and hits a bridge. A scaffolding pole that forms part of the bridges smashes through the windscreen, killing the passenger Joanne outright. Judy, in the driving seat, is largely unhurt, but is found to have drunk more than twice the legal limit for driving.

Along with themes of consequences, guilt and forgiveness, this is the exploration of how such a tragedy affects all those people – strangers and otherwise – who are suddenly thrown together in the aftermath of a violent and terrible event.

Mark Wheeller wrote the play using words spoken during interviews with all those involved in the incident. He contrasts this authentic dialogue with a number of stylized and Brechtian techniques including direct audience address, projected slides showing the accident scene, and juxtaposed moments of humour that involve tightly choreographed movement and mime. The play is performed simply with very few props and is usually presented by two male and two female actors who, apart from the character of Judy, take on all the roles in the play.

The play opens with a dynamic sequence that re-creates Judy and Joanne's drunken night out in an exaggerated and stylized way. A contrasting retrospective account of their childhood and youth follows, and leads into the sections printed here that re-create the accident and the events immediately afterwards, as the witness Duncan and the police constables attend the scene.

Introductory task

1.   In your group, create a series of four still images that show a group of young people enjoying a typical night out on the town. Make each image as dynamic and interesting to look at as possible. Attempt to make each image contrast with the last using levels, exaggerated body language and posture, and facial expression.

2. Now create a final image. There has been a drink-driving accident. Create your image of this as a direct contrast to the previous four images. Experiment with representing the accident in different ways – symbolically, or through the reaction of the witnesses, perhaps. Choose a piece of music and choreograph your sequence of changing still images to it.

Task 1

1. Look at Section 3: The Accident. In the stage directions, it says '*The accident is simulated stylistically somehow!!!*' In your group, discuss how you would represent the accident. Now read the Actor 1 and Actor 2 lines at the same time as Judy's lines. Experiment with whispering, chanting, and increasing the volume and intensity of the lines leading to the dramatic climax of the scene.

2. Place two chairs or blocks together to represent the car's seats. Shape an image around Joanne and Judy that will show the final impact and incorporates everyone. Work backwards now, exploring the movements that will get you to this final image. Consider repeated movements or symbolic gestures, sounds, claps or percussion. Use the language and words to give your sequence a rhythm. Try to use the specific music track mentioned, or alternatively a slow love ballad to contrast with the horror of the incident.

Task 2

1. Read through Section 4: The Aftermath. Read through Duncan's account of arriving first at the scene of the accident. Who is he speaking to? Is his language stylized or naturalistic?

2. Divide Duncan's opening speech among your group. Each actor should decide how to present his or her section. Place two chairs on stage to represent Judy and Joanne. Duncan acts as narrator, speaking directly to the audience as he describes what happened and what he did to try to help. Experiment with ways of stepping in and out of the drama and using mime to show his actions – looking out of the window, getting dressed, trying to open the car door. Perform the sequence with each actor following on and acting his or her section. Discuss which interpretations were effective.

Task 3

1. Read Duncan's section that starts *'I went back home and poured myself a great big bloody drink!'* Why do you think Duncan seems to be angry at this point? Who is he angry with?

2. Place a chair in the middle of your small group. Ask for a volunteer to take on the role of Duncan while the others hot-seat him by asking questions about his feelings from that night.

Cultural references

1. Discuss posters and adverts warning about drink-driving that you have seen. Which ones do you think are effective at discouraging people from drink-driving?

2. Drinking habits, especially among young people, are changing. Why do you think this is? What role does the alcoholic drinks industry have to play in shaping our behaviour?

Writing task

1. Based on your drama work on this extract, write a series of director's notes that describe two of the characters, and include advice about how to act out the roles. Consider voice, tone, body language, movement and posture and how the character might relate to the other characters on stage and to the audience during any direct address.

2. Write a local newspaper editorial reporting and commenting upon the incident. Take a standpoint as to what your newspaper thinks is a fitting punishment for Judy. Justify the newspaper's opinions. You can include expert witness statements or comments from other characters.

The Elephant Man

Bernard Pomerance

Characters in this extract

John Merrick	the Elephant Man
Frederick Treves	a surgeon and teacher
Carr Gomm	the administrator of the London hospital where Merrick is housed
Porter	at the London hospital
Snork	another porter
Mrs Kendal	an actress

Plot summary

The Elephant Man is based on the true story of John Merrick, who lived in London during the late 1800s. Merrick, a horribly deformed young man who has been a freak show attraction, is found abandoned and helpless. He is admitted to a prestigious London hospital for observation and there he meets Frederick Treves, a famous young doctor. Charged with Merrick's care, Treves educates him and introduces him to London society. Soon Merrick becomes a great favourite of the aristocracy and literati. But his belief that he can become a man like any other is a dream never to be realized.

Scene 8

MERCY AND JUSTICE ELUDE
OUR MINDS AND ACTIONS

Merrick *in bath.* Treves, Gomm.

Merrick	How long is as long as I like?
Treves	You may stay for life. The funds exist.
Merrick	Been reading this. About homes for the blind. Wouldn't mind going to one when I have to move.
Treves	But you do not have to move; and you're not blind.
Merrick	I would prefer it where no one stared at me.
Gomm	No one will bother you here.
Treves	Certainly not. I've given instructions.

Porter *and* **Snork** *peek in.*

Porter	What'd I tell you?
Snork	Gawd almighty. Oh. Mr Treves. Mr Gomm.
Treves	You were told not to do this. I don't understand. You must not lurk about. Surely you have work?
Porter	Yes, sir.
Treves	Well, it is infuriating. When you are told a thing, you must listen. I won't have you gaping in on my patients. Kindly remember that.
Porter	Isn't a patient, sir, is he?
Treves	Do not let me find you here again.
Porter	Didn't know you were here, sir. We'll be off now.
Gomm	No, no, Will. Mr Treves was precisely saying no one would intrude when you intruded.
Treves	He is warned now. Merrick does not like it.

Gomm	He was warned before. On what penalty, Will?
Porter	That you'd sack me, sir.
Gomm	You are sacked, Will. You, his friend, you work here?
Snork	Just started last week, sir.
Gomm	Well, I hope the point is taken now.
Porter	Mr Gomm – I ain't truly sacked, am I?
Gomm	Will, yes. Truly sacked. You will never be more truly sacked.
Porter	It's not me. My wife ain't well. My sister has got to take care of our kids, and of her. Well.
Gomm	Think of them first next time.
Porter	It ain't as if I interfered with his medicine.
Gomm	That is exactly what it is. You may go.
Porter	Just keeping him to look at in private. That's all. Isn't it?
	Snork *and* **Porter** *exit.*
Gomm	There are priorities, Frederick. The first is discipline. Smooth is the passage to the tight ship's master. Merrick, you are safe from prying now.
Treves	Have we nothing to say, John?
Merrick	If all that's stared at me'd been sacked – there'd be whole towns out of work.
Treves	I meant, 'Thank you, sir.'
Merrick	'Thank you, sir.'
Treves	We always do say please and thank you, don't we?
Merrick	Yes, sir. Thank you.
Treves	If we want to properly be like others.
Merrick	Yes, sir, I want to.

Treves   Then it is for our own good, is it not?

Merrick   Yes, sir, Thank you, Mr Gomm.

Gomm   Sir, you are welcome. [Exits.]

Treves   You are happy here, are you not, John?

Merrick   Yes.

Treves   The baths have rid you of the odour, have they not?

Merrick   First chance I had to bathe regular. Ly.

Treves   And three meals a day delivered to your room?

Merrick   Yes, sir.

Treves   This is your Promised Land is it not? A roof. Food. Protection. Care. Is it not?

Merrick   Right, Mr Treves.

Treves   I will bet you don't know what to call this.

Merrick   No, sir, I don't.

Treves   You call it, Home.

Merrick   Never had a home before.

Treves   You have one now. Say it, John: Home.

Merrick   Home.

Treves   No, no, really say it. I have a home. This is my home. Go on.

Merrick   I have a home. This is my home. This is my home. I have a home. As long as I like?

Treves   That is what home is.

Merrick   That is what home is.

Treves   If I abide by the rules, I will be happy.

Merrick   Yes, sir.

Treves   Don't be shy.

Merrick   If I abide by the rules I will be happy.

Treves   Very good. Why?

Merrick   Why what?

Treves   Will you be happy?

Merrick   Because it is my home?

Treves   No, no. Why do rules make you happy?

Merrick   I don't know.

Treves   Of course you do.

Merick   No, I really don't.

Treves   Why does anything make you happy?

Merrick   Like what? Like what?

Treves   Don't be upset. Rules make us happy because they are for our own good.

Merrick   Okay.

Treves   Don't be shy, John. You can say it.

Merrick   This is my home?

Treves   No. About rules making us happy.

Merrick   They make us happy because they are for our own good.

Treves   Excellent. Now: I am submitting a follow-up paper on you to the London Pathological Society. It would help if you told me what you recall about your first years, John. To fill in gaps.

Merrick   To fill in gaps. The workhouse where they put me. They beat you there like a drum. Boom boom: scrape the floor white. Shine the pan, boom boom. It never ends. The floor is always dirty. The pan is always tarnished. There is nothing you can do about it. You are always attacked anyway. Boom boom. Boom boom. Boom boom. Will the children go to the workhouse?

Treves   What children?

Merrick   The children. The man he sacked.

Treves   Of necessity. Will will find other employment. You don't want crowds staring at you. Do you?

Merrick   No.

Treves   In your own home you do not have to have crowds staring at you. Or anyone. Do you? In your home?

Merrick   No.

Treves   Then Mr Gomm was merciful. You yourself are proof. Is it not so? [*Pause.*] Well? Is it not so?

Merrick   If your mercy is so cruel, what do you have for justice?

Treves   I am sorry. It is just the way things are.

Merrick   Boom boom. Boom boom. Boom boom.

         Fadeout.

Scene 9

MOST IMPORTANT ARE WOMEN

Merrick *asleep, head on knees.* **Treves**, **Mrs Kendal** *foreground.*

Treves   You have seen photographs of John Merrick, Mrs Kendal. You are acquainted with his appearance.

Mrs Kendal   He reminds me of an audience I played Cleopatra for in Brighton once. All huge grim head and grimace and utterly unable to clap.

Treves   Well. My aim's to lead him to as normal a life as possible. His terror of us all comes from having been held at arm's length from society. I am determined that shall end. For example, he loves to meet people and converse. I am determined he shall. For example, he had never seen the inside of any normal home before. I had him to mine, and what a reward, Mrs Kendal; his astonishment, his joy at the most ordinary things. Most critical I feel, however, are women. I will explain. They have always shown the greatest fear and loathing of him. While he adores them of course.

Mrs Kendal Ah. He is intelligent.

Treves I am convinced they are the key to retrieving him from his exclusion. Though, I must warn you, women are not quite real to him – more creatures of his imagination.

Mrs Kendal Then he is already like other men, Mr Treves.

Treves So I thought, an actress could help. I mean, unlike most women, you won't give in, you are trained to hide your feelings and assume others.

Mrs Kendal You mean unlike most women I am famous for it that is really all.

Treves Well. In any case. If you could enter the room and smile and wish him good morning. And when you leave, shake his hand, the left one is usable, and really quite beautiful, and say, 'I am very pleased to have made your acquaintance, Mr Merrick.'

Mrs Kendal Shall we try it? Left hand out please. [*Suddenly radiant.*] I am *very* pleased to have made your acquaintance Mr Merrick. I am very *pleased* to have made your acquaintance Mr Merrick. I am very pleased to have made your *acquaintance* Mr Merrick. I *am* very pleased to have made *your* acquaintance Mr Merrick. Yes. That one.

Treves By god, they are all splendid. Merrick will be so pleased. It will be the day he becomes a man like other men.

Mrs Kendal Speaking of that, Mr Treves.

Treves Frederick, please.

Mrs Kendal Freddie, may I commit an indiscretion?

Treves Yes?

Mrs Kendal I could not but help noticing from the photographs that – well – of the unafflicted parts – ah, how shall I put it? [*Points to photograph.*]

Treves Oh. I see! I quite. Understand. No, no, no, it is quite normal.

Mrs Kendal   I thought as much.

Treves   Medically speaking, uhm, you see the papillomatous extrusions which disfigure him, uhm, seem to correspond quite regularly to the osseous deformities, that is, excuse me, there is a link between the bone disorder and the skin growths, though for the life of me I have not discovered what it is or why it is, but in any case this – part – it would be therefore unlikely to be afflicted because well, that is, well, there's no bone in it. None in it. None at all. I mean.

Mrs Kendal   Well. Learn a little every day don't we?

Treves   I am horribly embarrassed.

Mrs Kendal   Are you? Then he must be lonely indeed.

   Fadeout.

Scene 10

WHEN THE ILLUSION ENDS HE
MUST KILL HIMSELF

Merrick *sketching. Enter* **Treves, Mrs Kendal**.

Treves   He is making sketches for a model of St Phillip's church. He wants someday to make a model, you see.

   John, my boy, this is Mrs Kendal. She would very much like to make your acquaintance.

Mrs Kendal   Good morning Mr Merrick.

Treves   I will see to a few matters. I will be back soon. [*Exits.*]

Merrick   I planned so many things to say. I forget them. You are so beautiful.

Mrs Kendal   Good morning Mr Merrick.

Merrick   Well. Really that was what I planned to say. That I forgot what I planned to say. I couldn't think of anything else I was so excited.

Mrs Kendal   Real charm is always planned, don't you think?

Merrick   Well. I do not know why I look like this, Mrs Kendal. My mother was so beautiful. She was knocked down by an elephant in a circus while she was pregnant. Something must have happened, don't you think?

Mrs Kendal   It may well have.

Merrick   It may well have. But sometimes I think my head is so big because it is so full of dreams. Because it is. Do you know what happens when dreams cannot get out?

Mrs Kendal   Why no.

Merrick   I don't either. Something must. [*Silence.*] Well. You are a famous actress.

Mrs Kendal   I am not unknown.

Merrick   You must display yourself for your living then. Like I did.

Mrs Kendal   That is not myself, Mr Merrick. That is an illusion. This is myself.

Merrick   This is myself too.

Mrs Kendal   Frederick says you like to read. So: books.

Merrick   I am reading *Romeo and Juliet* now.

Mrs Kendal   Ah. Juliet. What a love story. I adore love stories.

Merrick   I like love stories best too. If I had been Romeo, guess what.

Mrs Kendal   What?

Merrick   I would not have held the mirror to her breath.

Mrs Kendal   You mean the scene where Juliet appears to be dead and he holds a mirror to her breath and sees –

Merrick   Nothing. How does it feel when he kills himself because he just sees nothing?

Mrs Kendal   Well. My experience as Juliet has been – particularly with an actor I will not name – that while I'm laying there dead dead dead, and he is lamenting excessively, I get to thinking that if this slab of ham does not part from the hamhock of his life toute suite, I am going to scream, pop off the tomb, and plunge a dagger into his scene-stealing heart. Romeos are very undependable.

Merrick   Because he does not care for Juliet.

Mrs Kendal   Not care?

Merrick   Does he take her pulse? Does he get a doctor? Does he make sure? He kills himself. The illusion fools him because he does not care for her. He only cares for himself. If I had been Romeo, we would have got away.

Mrs Kendal   But then there would be no play, Mr Merrick.

Merrick   If he did not lover her, why should there be a play? Looking in a mirror and seeing nothing. That is not love. It was an illusion. When the illusion ended he had to kill himself.

Mrs Kendal   Why. That is extraordinary.

Merrick   Before I spoke with people, I did not think of all these things because there was no one to bother to think them for. Now things just come out of my mouth which are true.

Treves enters.

Treves   You are famous, John. We are in the papers. Look. They have written up my report to the Pathological Society. Look — it is a kind of apotheosis for you.

Mrs Kendal   Frederick, I feel Mr Merrick would benefit from even more company than you provide; in fact by being acquainted with the best, and they with him. I shall make it my task if you'll permit. As you know, I am a friend of nearly everyone, and I do pretty well as I please and what pleased me is this task, I think.

Treves   By god, Mrs Kendal, you are splendid.

Mrs Kendal   Mr Merrick I must go now. I should like to return if I may. And so that we may without delay teach you about society, I would like to bring my good friend Dorothy Lady Neville. She would be most pleased if she could meet you. Let me tell her yes? [**Merrick** nods yes.] Then until next time. I'm sure your church model will surprise us all. Mr Merrick, it has been a very great pleasure to make your acquaintance.

Treves   John. Your hand. She wishes to shake your hand.

Merrick   Thank you for coming.

Mrs Kendal   But it was my pleasure. Thank you. [*Exits, accompanied by* **Treves**.]

Treves   What a wonderful success. Do you know he's never shaken a woman's hand before?

As lights fade **Merrick** *sobs soundlessly, uncontrollably.*

Context of the play

The Elephant Man is based on the true story of Joseph (John) Merrick, born in Leicester in 1862. Grossly deformed, Merrick became an exhibit in a travelling 'freak show', eventually meeting up with Frederick Treves, an eminent London doctor who found him sanctuary in the London Hospital, where he stayed until his death in 1890.

The play is remarkable in that no attempt is made to realistically portray Merrick's disfigurement or speech and mobility problems. Unlike the successful David Lynch film of the same name, Pomerance's play uses a stylized form of presentation that relies upon the power of an audience's imagination to create the image of Merrick.

Again unlike the Lynch film, the play focuses on Treves and other characters who come into contact with Merrick as he becomes something of a celebrity in Victorian London. A theme of the play is the way in which people in contact with Merrick recognize something about themselves: Merrick becomes a kind of 'mirror' reflecting the strengths and weaknesses of others.

In this extract (three consecutive scenes from the middle of the play) Merrick is installed in his hospital annexe in relative security. When a hospital porter is sacked for repeatedly peeking at Merrick, it is Merrick who feels empathy for the man's predicament, having spent time himself in a brutal workhouse. Treves seems unable to treat Merrick as an equal; he patronizes him like a child. But he arranges for Merrick to be visited by a beautiful actress, Mrs Kendal, and in the two subsequent scenes, it is Mrs Kendal who recognizes something in Merrick that Treves fails to comprehend.

Introductory task

In this sequence Treves insists that Merrick should express gratitude for the 'charity' he has received.

Imagine that the story of the 'Elephant Man' and his mentor has just been released to the press. Assume the role of present-day journalists, with one of the group assuming the role of Frederick Treves. Question him as to his motives for wanting to help Merrick. Do you think that journalists of the 1880s might have different attitudes towards Treves' 'charity'?

Task 1

1. In Scene 8, Merrick describes an impression of his past life in the workhouse where they beat him 'like a drum'. While two members of the group rehearse the sequence between Treves and Merrick which begins 'Now: I am submitting a follow up paper...' the rest of the group should create a montage of images – with percussion if you feel it appropriate – which represents Merrick's horrific memory of his past.

2. Run the sequence, and as Merrick performs his short monologue, experiment with finding interesting ways in which he can 'travel back' into his past (as represented by the other members of the group). What is the dramatic effect of adding images and sound to the sequence?

3. What do you think is intended by the last line of the scene? Is there a way in which the repeated 'boom boom' might be emphasized?

Task 2

In Scene 9 Treves and Mrs Kendal 'rehearse' her prospective meeting with Merrick. (This is perhaps an interesting parallel with another extract in this collection – Brecht's *Arturo Ui*, where Ui also consults an actor – for a rather different purpose.)

Throughout this and the following scene there are a number of references to the theatre, and to the idea of performance ('display') and 'illusion'. This seems to link with the idea that appearances can be deceptive and beauty is only skin deep. Create a dramatic sequence that illustrates what you understand by these sayings. Include – as spoken text – appropriate lines from the script.

Cultural references

Young people today are under considerable pressure to conform to an ideal – often unattainable – of what it is to be beautiful. The play raises a number of issues in relation to beauty, disability, and what 'humanity' really means.

Can you think of examples of contemporary figures who demonstrate real humanity in spite of a disability? Where do our assumptions about, and attitude towards disability come from?

Writing task

At the end of this sequence the lights go down on Merrick sobbing 'uncontrollably'. What emotions do you think he is feeling? Imagine that Merrick has tried to write down his feelings in the form of a poem. Write the poem.

Metamorphosis

Kafka adapted by Steven Berkoff

Characters in this extract

Gregor	a young travelling salesman who hates his job
Mr Samsa	Gregor's father
Mrs Samsa	Gregor's mother
Greta	Gregor's sister
Chief Clerk	Gregor's employer

Plot summary

Travelling salesman Gregor Samsa oversleeps one morning and wakes up to find that he has been transformed into a giant insect. Gregor's sisters, Greta, takes a practical approach to the problem, but soon she and her parents have to find work to survive. Gradually the family dynamic begins to disintegrate until, finally, a neglected and misunderstood Gregor dies.

In this extract, Gregor discovers his transformation. Although he dislikes his job, Gregor must work to support his family. When his employer arrives at the house to find out why Gregor is not at work, Gregor makes a huge effort – not easy in his transformed state – to get out of bed and open the bedroom door.

The family enters one at a time — backcloth lit — figures appear in silhouette. Each one enters in the character he or she is going to play, and performs a small mime condensing the personality into a few seconds. **Mother** *is first — describes a sad face — leaves a pained heart and angst.* **Father** *next strolls boldly on in boots and costume of mid-European lower middle-class tradesman — trousers in socks — and braces — no jacket, looking like Hindenburg. Then* **Greta**, *as student with violin. Then* **Gregor**, *who just walks on and smiles — an amiable being.*

As each speaks they form a line behind each other. On the last line they take on the movement of an insect by moving their arms to a particular rhythm. As no front lighting is used, this has the effect of an insect's leg movements.

Mr. S	[*enters*] As Gregor Samsa awoke one morning from uneasy dreams …
Mrs. S	[*enters*] He found himself transformed in his bed into a gigantic insect …
Greta	[*enters*] His numerous legs, which were pitifully thin compared to the rest of his bulk, waved helplessly before him.
	[*Movement starts.* **Gregor** *is in front. Suddenly the movement stops —* **Family** *dissolve the beetle image by moving away — leaving* **Gregor** *still moving as part of the insect image.*] [*Front lights come up revealing* **Family**.]
Gregor	What has happened to me?
Family	He thought.
Gregor	It was no dream.
Greta	[*as clock*] He looked at the alarm clock ticking on the chest.
Gregor	Half pas six and the hands were quietly moving on.
Mrs. S	Gregor, Gregor?
Mr. S	Said a voice.
Gregor	That gentle voice …
Greta	It was his mother's …
Mr. S	His mother's …
Mrs. S	His mother's …

[Fade.]

[Slow Tick] *[Lights snap up on the centre area downstage revealing* **Gregor** *standing behind* **Greta** *— scenes of pre-insect life. Each speak their own thoughts which run contrapuntally.]*

Gregor *[indicates]* I'm Gregor Samsa – there's my sister Greta.

Greta *[motionless]* There's brother Gregor.

Gregor Isn't that nice that she waits up for me.

Greta I always wait up for him.

Gregor Glass of milk on the table then bed – up again at four a.m. Yes four a.m.! To catch the five a.m. train.

Greta He doesn't come home often.

Gregor Daily! What a life – what an exhausting job, and I picked it.

Greta He works so hard.

Gregor I picked it? I'm a commercial traveller in the cloth trade – I have to work to keep them.

[Lights snap on downstage left and right revealing **Mother** *and* **Father** *both frozen.]*

Greta But he also makes things at home.

Gregor Who else can do it? Father's ill so they rely on me totally.

Greta He recently made a picture frame and in it he put a picture cut out of an illustrated magazine.

Gregor On my back it rests – their fortunes rest on my back like a great weight.

Greta It shows a lady with a fur cap and fur stole sitting upright and holding out to the spectator a huge fur muff into which the whole of her forearm had vanished.

[Image of above – music.]

Gregor The warehouse was better – one didn't have to worry about the travelling.

Greta It was very good.

Gregor   I feel sick.

[*Dissolve.*]

[*A loud ticking is heard which continues throughout the next scene — **Gregor** marches behind his **Family** who in time to the ticking call out **Gregor's** meaning for them. Double time for **Gregor** going about his work.*]

Greta   Gregor!

Mr. S   Cash!

Greta   Gregor!

Mr. S   Shoes!

Greta   Gregor!

Mr. S   Cigars!

Greta   Gregor!

Mrs. S   Food!

Greta   Gregor!

Mr. S   Beer!

Greta   Gregor!

Mrs. S   Clothes!

[*As **Gregor** comes to stop behind **Greta** — **Family** mime actions of domestic life in time to ticking resembling those automatic figures in wax-works — they repeat some combinations of gestures — only when they speak, do they freeze the movement.*]

Greta   Milk, Gregor?

[*Image — actors and marionette. **Father** smokes cigar and drinks. **Mother** sews. **Greta** reads her school books.*]

Gregor   Thanks — you're up late, why aren't you in bed?

Greta   I thought I'd wait up for you. What's the matter?

Gregor   My back's aching — must be carrying these samples all day.

[*Freeze action during next five speeches.*]

Mrs. S   Did you sell much?

Gregor   Not as much as last week.

Mr. S   [*disappointed*] Oh! – never mind – it'll be better tomorrow.

Gregor   Perhaps.

Mr. S   Of course it will.

[*Continue action.*]

Gregor   Ssh ... listen ...

Greta   What?

Gregor   It's raining again – hear it beating on the window gutter?

Mrs. S   [*listening*] It's been raining for ages.

Gregor   Oh God! [*Sits down wearily.*]

Greta   What is it?

Gregor   I'm so exhausted.

Mr. S   Go to bed then.

Gregor   Always tired – travelling day in, day out.

[*Image – the feet of the* **Family** *race while they sit – faces reveal the agony of* **Gregor's** *life – they become chorus for his statements.*]

On top of worry about train connections – snatching odd meals, (and if I arrive late at some small town, trudging the streets looking for an hotel). [*Repeat this sentence twice, once fast, once slow.*]

Mr. S   I thought you preferred it to the warehouse.

Gregor   Not any more – a man needs his sleep.

Greta   Well, go to bed then.

Gregor   [*ignoring her*] The other travellers have it easy – they're still at breakfast when

I've returned with the morning's orders.

[*Image of above — music.*]

Sometimes it's still dark out when I leave and the mornings are so empty and bitterly cold … I think that's why I've got a stiff back.

Greta   Why don't you leave?

Gregor   I will one day — rest assured, as soon as I've paid off father's debt to him, I'll go right up to the chief himself and tell him what I think of him.

Greta   [*giggling*] Oh that would be fun — imagine his face.

[*Image —* **Father's** *image of* **Chief Clerk**]

Gregor   It would knock him sideways if I did that …

[*Image of* **Clerk** *— tilting sideways.*]

He's such a strange little man … he's got an irritating habit of sitting high at his desk and talking down to me — and I have to crane my neck because he's hard of hearing.

Greta   Is there much to pay off?

Gregor   It should take another five years.

Mrs. S   Oh! As long as that!

Gregor   Then I'll cut myself loose!

Greta   Good, and if you're lucky it might be sooner.

Gregor   And that's another thing — you're always making casual acquaintances.

[*Image of* **Family** *going to meet and then parting, never quite succeeding in the act — music.*]

And before you've time to become friends you're off again. [*Moves his joints in time to ticking … first intimations of insect state.*] I don't know what's happening to me — all my joints feel stiff.

Greta   Perhaps you shouldn't go in tomorrow — don't go in — I'll get a doctor for you in the morning.

Mr. S }	
Mrs. S }	NO!

Greta   Why not?

Mr. S   It would look suspicious.

Gregor   I've not had a day's illness in five years.

Mr. S   The Chief Clerk himself would come here with the insurance doctor and put it all down to laziness.

Gregor   I mean I feel quite well really so they wouldn't be wrong, would they?

Greta   But you look so tired and pale.

Mr. S   That's the penalty for being a good salesman.

Family   *Oh Gregor, you're so good to us!*

Mr. S   You go to bed now.

Greta   And have a good night's sleep.

Mrs. S   And I'll make you a lovely breakfast in the morning.

Gregor   I could sleep forever. [*Moves slowly back to cage.*] Goodnight, Greta. [*Collapses into cage which is unlit – he is on his back motionless.*]

Family   [*in harmony*] Goodnight, Gregor.

[*Blackout.*]

[*Fast ticking starts – day begins. A hard light snaps on downstage – everything works by the clock – movements again are purely functional, speech patterns are geared to movement and ticking.*]

[*Cyclorama lit in white –* **Family** *in three white spots.* **Gregor** *a black silhouette, feet up – arm moving in and out.*]

[*Image –* **Family** *at breakfast,* **Gregor** *on his back, the still stiff insect before waking.*]

[*The mime of* **Family** *eating, looking up, wondering where* **Gregor** *is, in unison linked as a chorus.*]

Mr. S   It's half past six. Where's Gregor?

Mrs. S   Half past six — Oh dear — perhaps the alarm clock's not gone off.

Mr. S   Did you set it?

Greta   Set it? Yes. I set it for four o'clock.

Mr. S
Mrs. S   } Four o'clock.

Greta   I set it properly.

Mr. S   That ear-splitting noise should have woken him.

[*They move back on stools.*]

Mrs. S   Gregor? [*sung*] Oh Gregor? It's a quarter to seven already — shouldn't you have been at work?

Gregor   Yes — yes — thank you, Mother — I'm getting up now.

[*The ticking stops suddenly — the silence accentuates the stillness — their world of eating and normality ceases. They move now in very slow motion beginning to show anguish.*]

[*Image —* **Family** *silently mouth their concern. They hold gestures in listening.*]

What's happened to me — everything seems the same — it's still raining outside — Oh, my leg — what's wrong with my legs? Turn over and go back to sleep, it's a bad dream — I can't turn over — I can't turn!

[**Family** *turn on stools complete circles rather than walking up to his area. The stools are metal with shiny tops.*]

Family   Gregor!

Gregor   Shut my eyes — I'm dreaming. [*to his legs and arms as if wishing them to dissolve*] Go away! It's nonsense — it must go away — spots on my belly? Ooh! They're itching. [*Scratches furiously.*] Must sleep — but I can't sleep on my back!

[**Family** *turn other way on stools — their faces return showing anxiety — 'Never has he been late before' — expression of dismay, fear, wonderment.*]

Family   Gregor!

[*Interjections become more frequent from* **Family**.]

Gregor   I have to work – it's quarter to seven – why didn't I hear the alarm – the next train goes at seven and my samples are not even packed and even if I caught the train there'd be a row – I knew I was sick yesterday.

[**Family** turn different directions on stools like computer wheels.]

Greta   Gregor – aren't you feeling well? Are you needing something?

Gregor   I'm just ready – won't be a minute.

Greta   Open the door, Gregor – please do.

Gregor   Yes, soon – soon.

[Very loud knock on door, the **Family** rise.]

[Three loud knocks followed by the **Chief Clerk** who makes a long entrance while the Family speak – sharing the next speech.]

[Image – they repeat this speech once still, once in panic – figure of eight round stools.]

Mr. S   Oh dear – that's bound to be somebody from the warehouse/

Greta   The porter would have reported his failure to turn up/

Mrs. S   That porter was the boss's boot-licker, spineless and stupid/it's sure to be him . . .

Clerk   [enters] No, Mr. Samsa, it's the Chief Clerk.

[**Family** all sit in shock]

Young Mr Samsa's not been in this morning – [**Chief Clerk** doffs imaginary hat – he walks along the line of the **Family** to **Mrs. S** from stage L to R.] Ah, Mrs Samsa, good morning – thought I'd drop round, see what the trouble is.

[Pause – silence as they turn to face **Chief Clerk**.]

Gregor   [slow] Snoop . . . Chief Clerk himself.

[**Chief Clerk** wears steel-tipped tap shoes so the can tap the floor like an impatient clock – he taps the floor until **Mrs. S** says 'I'm terribly sorry' since there is a pause that allows that impatience.]

Mrs. S   I'm terribly sorry, but our son's not feeling well – I don't quite know what's wrong – it's very unlike him – he's very conscientious as you know – thinks of nothing but his work.

[**Chief Clerk** *moves menacingly in from L. They turn slowly. The* **Family** *shrink back on their chairs – freeze in attitudes of fear and oppression by authority represented by the* **Chief Clerk**.]

Clerk   Hmmm!

[*Image –* **Family** *threatened by* **Chief Clerk**.]

Gregor   What a villain – it is impossible to be a couple of hours late without sending the Chief Clerk himself to investigate – giving my family something fresh to worry about, it'll soon go away – like those little pains I had, caused by awkward postures which soon disappeared then I woke up. [*Starts rocking.*] Mustn't hit my head . . . mustn't lose consciousness now.

[**Chief Clerk** *moves now to stage L in front of and round stool and now oppresses* **Mr. Samsa**.]

Mrs. S   Gregor! The Chief Clerk's here!

Greta   He's worried.

Mr. S   Why you are not at work.

[**Chief Clerk** *is now on stage L.* **Family** *shrink in opposite position and freeze.*]

Gregor   I know, I know. I only want to get up quietly without disturbing anyone, put my clothes on, and have my breakfast. [**Gregor**, *who has been on his back the whole time, now attempts to shift to his front.*] Must push – push – harder – Harder. [*Thumps over completely on his front.*]

[**Family** *sit bolt upright after crash.*]

Clerk   Sounds like someone fell in the next room.

[**Mr. and Mrs. Samsa** *thread these next speeches inside each other,* **Mr. Samsa** *walking up and down stage with* **Greta** *punctuating the odd 'Gregor'. Whilst downstage* **Mrs. Samsa** *attempts to smooth the* **Chief Clerk's** *fears. This is the first time the* **Family** *actually move to his room area. Movements are steady. Symmetrical, beating, harmonious patterns – not yet driven into confusion, more concerned.*]

[*Image – ordered confusion as they walk to cage and* **Chief Clerk** *eats* **Gregor's** *breakfast.*]

[**Mr. Samsa** *and* **Greta** *move to* **Gregor's** *area. A synonymous pattern emerges – they freeze on the point of impact, on the end of* **Mrs. Samsa's** *speech – a split second pause – a picture – frozen – of concern.*]

Mr. S	Excuse me. [*Goes to* **Gregor's** *room.*] Gregor – the Chief Clerk himself has come down to see you.
Greta	Gregor.
Mrs. S	He's not really well, believe me. [*Freeze.*]
Mr. S	Wants to know why you didn't go in today.
Mrs. S	What else would make him miss the train? [*Freeze.*]
Mr. S	We don't know what to say to him.
Greta	Gregor.
Mrs. S	He thinks of nothing but his work. [*Freeze.*]
Greta	Gregor.
Mr. S	Besides, he wants to talk to you privately.
Greta	Gregor.
Mrs. S	It makes me almost cross the way he never goes out in the evenings. [*Freeze.*]
Greta	Gregor.
Mr. S	So please open the door.
Mrs. S	Dancing and things like that.
Mr. S	He won't mind if your room's untidy.
Mrs. S	He just sits and reads or studying the railway timetables. [*Freeze.*]
Greta	[*to* **Gregor**] Please Gregor – you'll get in trouble.
Mrs. S	[*to* **Clerk**] The only amusement he gets is doing fretwork – do you know he spent three evenings cutting out a lovely picture frame – he's very clever with his hands … I'm sure he's unwell … it's not like him.
Clerk	I can't think of any other explanation, madam – and while I hope it's not

serious, I must say that in business one must ignore slight indispositions — work must go on.

Mrs. S   Oh yes, I absolutely agree — well I hope it's not slight … [*One movement reaction from* **Family** *amplifying her statement.*] I mean not serious … [*Repeat.*] … [*Breaks off not knowing what to say.*] Oh, I don't know.

Mr. S   [*knocking at the door*] Gregor. Once and for all. Will you let the Chief Clerk in?

Gregor   Leave me in peace!

[*There is a shocked silence.* **Mr. Samsa** *moves away in gesture of bewilderment, fear, puzzlement as the* **Chief Clerk** *comes to take his place at the door.*]

[**Family** *listen in frozen/intent.*]

Clerk   [*trying door*] Mr Samsa — what is the matter with you — why have you barricaded yourself in your room, just answering yes and no all the time — causing your good parents a great deal of trouble and neglecting your business duties in an incredible fashion? [*Silence.*] You amaze me — you really amaze me — I always thought you quiet and dependable and now you seem bent on making a disgraceful exhibition of yourself. The Chief did hint that a possible explanation for your disappearance was the funds that you were entrusted with.

[*Image —* **Family** *outrage and opposition.*]

Family   Oh no!

Clerk   I, of course, defended you, but seeing your behaviour now makes me doubt the wisdom of my actions!

Mr. S   He's an honest boy!

Mrs. S   He'd never do that!

Greta   Never! Oh Gregor, open the door please.

[*They incline heads in — no response — move downstage slowly and thoughtfully.*]

[*Image — what to do? Hands flapping behind backs.*]

[**Chief Clerk** *moves downstage — even his authority has failed.* **Greta** *rushes to* **Father** *— who pats her encouragingly as she starts to cry.* **Chief Clerk** *and* **Mother** *looks at* **Mr. Samsa**, *who expressed helplessness.*]

Clerk	Do you have another key?
Greta	Another key – I don't think so.
Mrs. S	We've never needed more than one key before.
Clerk	Does he always lock himself in?

[*They search for key.*]

Mrs. S	He never used to – it's a habit he got into through travelling in strange hotels – he said that you should always lock the door at night – he's very prudent like that.
Clerk	[*getting exasperated*] I intended to discuss with him in private but as he's wasted my time I don't see why I should … for some time past his work at the firm has not come up to scratch, Mr. Samsa, and this can't go on much longer.
Gregor	[*Crying out – a guttural voice – a creature less than a human – his words become less and less distinguishable to them. They all rush to the door.*] Sir, I'm just going to open the door – this very minute … slight illness – an attack of giddiness – kept me in my bed – getting up now – just a moment longer – sudden attack – be as right as rain soon – no foundations in your reports – no-one said anything to me – obviously you haven't looked at my last order – spare my parents – I'll catch the eight o'clock train – Don't let me detain you – please make my excuses to the Chief.

[*Image – total **Family** confusion – figures twist and whirl around each other like a frenetic dance.*]

Clerk	[*Rushing downstage – **Family's** movement becomes faster and faster as confusion breaks loose.*] Did you make out a word of it – is he trying to make fools of us?
Mrs. S	[*moving downstage with **Greta***] Oh dear, perhaps he's terribly ill and we're tormenting him.
Mr. S	My son has never behaved like this.
Clerk	No respect.
Mrs. S	Greta!
Greta	Yes Mother.

Mrs. S   Gregor is ill – go for a doctor.

Mr. S   My son – open the door.

Clerk   The man's mad.

Mrs. S   Go quickly.

Mr. S   My son!

Mrs. S   [to **Chief Clerk**] Did you hear how he was speaking?

Clerk   It was almost inhuman!

Mr. S   And get a locksmith, Greta – quick as you can!

Mrs. S   I'll boil a kettle.

           [*Image* – **Family** *frozen in anguish mixed with determination.*]

Context of the play

Franz Kafka wrote *The Metamorphosis* in 1912, a short novel about Gregor Samsa, who sacrifices his happiness to provide for his family. Transformed into an enormous beetle, Gregor becomes a burden to his family, helplessly trapped in his room watching them turn against him as his condition worsens.

Steven Berkoff's adaptation of Kafka's novella was first performed in 1969. Its figurative mime, music, choreography, choral and ensemble acting with stylized physical and vocal characterizations make significant demands upon any acting company. Berkoff's 'Total Theatre' approach to performance places the actor at the centre of the theatrical experience. Props, costumes and set are minimal so that the ensemble cast can focus the audience's attention upon the story. As well as experimenting with vocal and choral techniques, actors need to explore the play's stage directions and implied physical action.

Introductory task

1.   Gregor's altered state is symbolic and reflects his feelings about his life. In groups, find clues that suggest Gregor is unhappy. Does this explain why he has changed?

2.   As a small group, imagine you are a team of medical experts who have been researching Gregor's case. Devise a short presentation in role that details your findings and presents your theories explaining this medical mystery. In your presentation, include some key lines from the play as evidence.

Task 1

1.   Read through the stage directions at the start of the extract. The Samsa family are introduced by distilling each character's personality into a stylized movement or gesture. Working in a group of four, write down the names of the Samsa family. Underneath each name, write some adjectives that you think describe their appearance and personality.

2.   Choose a character to represent. In pairs, allow your partner to 'sculpt' your body and face into a position or aspect that he or she thinks best suits your character. Then swap over.

Task 2

1. Discuss how an actor playing Gregor might capture the physical and emotional state of being trapped in a beetle's body, without costumes or props.

2. The first beetle appearance is presented as an ensemble image focusing on the movement of insect legs. In your group, read through the opening dialogue. Now look at the stage directions. Experiment with different ways of creating the beetle's legs. Try contrasting movements that are fluid, fragmented or angular, with a range of different tempos. How does the narration help the scene? Who is it directed at? What relationship does this set up between the audience and the actors?

Task 3

1. Create a still image of Gregor as the beetle as the family eat their breakfast. Rehearse this section, following the stage directions closely. How can the movements of the family reflect the growing fear and anxiety of Gregor? Experiment with repeated movements, different movements or movements that cannon into each other and grow in intensity.

Cultural references

Write down a list of things that might contribute to feelings of stress in modern life. How do people deal with their busy lives? What can happen if the coping strategies fail?

Writing task

1. The attitude of Gregor's family changes towards him as they realize Gregor will no longer be able to provide for them. How might each person react? Which character will change the most in the way he or she views Gregor's condition? Write a series of short diary accounts as Mr Samsa, Mrs Samsa or Greta documenting their feelings over the first few days and weeks of Gregor's transformation.

2. Based on your drama work on this extract, write director's notes for Gregor. Include advice on how an actor might physically represent the beetle including vocal and movement quality.

Brokenville

Philip Ridley

Characters in this extract

Old Woman	female, in her 80s
Child	male, 10 years old
Bruise	female, 15 years old
Glitter	female, 14 years old
Tattoo	male, 15 years old
Quiff	male, 14 years old
Satchel	male, 16 years old

Plot summary

A city has been destroyed by disaster and lies in ruins, through which a young child wanders alone, clutching a music box and a book of fairy tales. As the child falls asleep, the sound of the music box attracts others to the place, none of whom can remember anything about themselves or what has happened to them.

When the child awakes and begins to panic, an old woman encourages calm. The group begin to tell stories to comfort the child, and in doing so start to confront what has happened and to piece their lives back together.

Child *points.*

Old Woman   *What?*

Child *still points.*

Bruise   Something over here.

Goes to some shelves.

The vase?

Child *shakes his head.*

Bruise   This?

Holds up broken piece of mirror. **Child** *nods.*

Glitter   What is it?

Bruise   A piece of mirror.

Child *sits in front of fire.*

Old Woman   [*at* **Bruise**] You know what to do.

Bruise *goes to fire.*

Others gather around her.

Slight pause.

Bruise   There was once a …

Glitter   Princess Glitter?

Bruise   No.

Tattoo   King Tattoo?

Bruise   Yes.

Slight pause.

But he was a blind King.

Tattoo   Why?

Bruise   Because you once had a Queen. And you didn't show her enough love. The Queen died of a broken heart. And, once she was dead, you realised just how much you really cared for her. You cried your eyes out.

Child claps excitedly.

Bruise   Every day the King walked in the garden of the Castle.

Old Woman   The garden belonged to your dead Queen.

Bruise   And the smell of her flowers – yes! It brings you comfort.

Tattoo   But I can't see it, right?

Glitter   Your son describes it to you.

Slight pause.

Old Woman   Prince Quiff?

Quiff   I thought the Prince was dead.

Old Woman   New story, new Prince.

Tattoo puts hand on Quiff's shoulder.

Child claps with delight.

Tattoo   Describe the garden, Prince Quiff.

Quiff   Oh … it's not bad. Yellow climbing flowers – Oh, what they called?

Tattoo   Roses?

Quiff   That's it! Roses! All over the walls. And they're all around the border too. And the blue rose tree in each corner. There. How's that?

Old Woman   Very good.

Glitter   Yes. Good.

Bruise   There was nothing King Tattoo liked to do more than sit in the dead Queen's garden and … smell the roses.

Tattoo sniffs.

Tattoo   ... Very flowery.

Slight pause.

Bruise   And then, one day, a Dragon flew out of the sky.

Old Woman   [*at* **Child**] They're scary, those Dragons.

Satchel   Where did it come from?

Old Woman   From ... from the nearby mountains.

*Child whispers in **Old Woman's** ear.*

Old Woman   Good point. [*at* **Bruise**] Why hadn't anyone seen the Dragon before?

Bruise   Because ... because the Dragon hadn't smelt the roses. That's it. You see, the roses had been growing and growing. More and more every year. And now ... well, the Castle was full of them. And ... there's nothing Dragons like more than to eat roses. But, King Tattoo didn't want the Dragon to eat his garden so ...

Tattoo   I'll see Wizard Satchel. [*at* **Child**] Right?

Child nods approvingly.

Tattoo goes to Satchel.

Tattoo   That Dragon's going to munch my garden. Do something.

Satchel   The Dragon's not greedy. Take my advice. Give it a corner of your garden. Grow roses just for the Dragon. I'm sure it'll be happy and leave the rest of your garden alone.

Tattoo   I'm not having that overgrown lizard stomping around like he owns the place. Where's my son? Prince!

Slight pause.

Prince Quiff!

Quiff   Oh ... sorry! Here! Wotcha, King Tatt.

Tattoo   Kill the Dragon. And don't call me Tatt.

Quiff   But Wiz Satch just said –

Tattoo   No 'buts'. It's an order. Chop the Dragon's head off.

Quiff   It only wants a few bushes.

Tattoo   Not one petal.

Slight pause.

Bruise   So … Prince Quiff got the biggest sword he could find and went to the mountains.

Slight pause.

Old Woman   Go on.

Bruise   [with **Glitter**] Chop-chop!

Glitter   [with **Bruise**] Chop-chop!

Quiff   If this messes up my quiff, there'll be trouble.

Quiff *picks up table leg and starts climbing pile of rubble.*

Quiff   Dragon!

Old Woman   Louder.

Quiff   Dragon!

Satchel   Louder!

Quiff   Dragon! Dragon! Dragon!

Bruise   Then he saw something. On top of the mountain. It was very large and … made of twigs.

Quiff   What is it?

Old Woman   You're the one up the mountain.

Quiff   … A nest.

Bruise   Anything inside?

Quiff   Eggs.

Old Woman   How many?

Quiff   Nine.

　　　　*Child whimpers in **Old Woman's** ear.*

Old Woman   Describe them.

Quiff   They're huge. All different colours. Glittering. More beautiful than anything I've ever seen.

　　　　Child claps approvingly.

Bruise   And that's when the Dragon attacked.

Quiff   Why?

Bruise   Protecting its nest.

Quiff   I'm not hurting it.

Satchel   Dragon don't know that.

Bruise   The Prince stabbed the Dragon.

Quiff   Take that!

Bruise   The Dragon chased Prince Quiff back down the mountain.

Quiff   Mind my quiff, you Dragon.

　　　　Descends rubble.

　　　　You can't beat me! Look at my muscles. My stomach. Six-pack or what?

Glitter   Oh, get on with it.

　　　　Quiff swings table leg.

Quiff   There!

Bruise   What you done?

Quiff   Chopped its head off.

Picks up a piece of rubble.

See – ! Oh, it's a heavy head.

Bruise Take it to the King.

Quiff *drops rubble in front of* **Tattoo**.

Quiff Look at it, Dad! Well, you can't. You're blind. But if you could – why, you'd see the head of the scariest Dragon ever. But I – yes, me! Prince Quiff! – I fought it and won. No problem! What a fight it was.

Tattoo You did a good job, son.

Quiff The Dragon didn't stand a chance against my muscles.

Old Woman But the Prince had to forget the Dragon.

Quiff Why?

Glitter Time to grow up.

Bruise And marry.

Quiff Marry!

Old Woman A Princess!

Glitter … Me?

Quiff Who'd want to marry you? Not me!

Glitter And who'd want to marry you? Not me!

Bruise King Tattoo will decide.

Tattoo Get hitched, you two.

Slight pause.

Glitter *takes a step towards* **Quiff**.

Old Woman Closer.

Glitter *takes another step.*

Old Woman Closer. [*at* **Quiff**] You too!

Quiff *takes a step.*

Glitter *takes a step.*

Eventually, they stand next to each other.

Satchel   The Prince and Princess are married!

Throws torn paper like confetti.

Others cheer and clap.

Slight pause.

Old Woman   Honeymoon!

Glitter   [with **Quiff**] Honeymoon?

Quiff   [with **Glitter**] Honeymoon?

Slight pause.

Quiff   Wotcha, Princess.

Glitter   Wotcha, Prince

Old Woman   Kiss!

Glitter   [with **Quiff**] Do what?

Quiff   [with **Glitter**] Do what?

Satchel   Snog time!

Quiff   But I don't fancy her!

Glitter   And I don't fancy him!

Old Woman   It's for the story.

Quiff and Glitter stare at each other awkwardly.

Gradually they lean towards each other.

Just as it looks as if they might actually kiss –

Glitter   The garden!

Quiff	Wh … what?
Glitter	Bit of a make-over, I think.
Quiff	The King won't like you changing things.
Glitter	I can't think about kissing till I've made this garden my own. We can have some yellow roses over there. And some orange ones over here. And just here – those roses with different-coloured petals.

Slight pause.

Quiff	Did I tell you about the Dragon?
Glitter	Zillions of times.
Quiff	I fought and fought it. My sword went right in his eye. Yellow jelly spurted out.
Glitter	Do you like this rose?
Quiff	I stabbed the other eye.
Glitter	This rose?
Quiff	More yellow jelly?
Glitter	What are you playing at? How we gonna move the story forward if you keep – Oh, you're so … so …
Quiff	Gorgeous?

Glitter squeals in desperation.

Tattoo	What's wrong, Princess Glitter?
Glitter	I'm not doing it with him!
Quiff	[laughing] Doing it?
Glitter	You've got a mind like a sewer! Oh, I never wanted to marry.
Old Woman	So what do you want?

Slight pause.

Bruise whispers in *Glitter's* ear.

Glitter looks at Bruise, unsure.

Bruise nods.

Glitter   ... A baby.

Quiff   No way!

Bruise   So the King went to –

Satchel   Wizard Satchel here!

Quiff   I don't want a baby.

Tattoo   What can be done, Wizard Satchel?

Quiff   I don't want a baby.

Old Woman   You do!

Quiff   I don't!

Bruise   [with **Old Woman**] You do!

Glitter   [with **Old Woman**] You do!

Slight pause.

Old Woman   Why don't you make a mirror, Wizard Satchel?

*Bruise gives mirror to **Satchel**.*

Satchel   A mirror! Right! Good idea. Well ... it's a magic mirror, obviously. Now ... what can it do?

Tattoo   Don't you know?

Satchel   There's lots of spells, you know.

Slight pause.

Got it! Take this mirror to Prince Quiff. When he looks in it, he'll forget all about the Dragon.

*Gives mirror to **Tattoo**.*

Tattoo   So ... what? The Prince has to look into this all day. That's the spell?

Satchel   Got it! Gradually, break off tiny bits of the mirror. So small the Prince won't see. And keep doing that till the mirror's all gone. By that time … well, the Prince will have forgotten about the Dragon altogether. There! How's that?

Tattoo   It'll do.

Satchel   One more thing. Don't look into the mirror yourself.

Tattoo   I can't! I'm blind!

Satchel   Then there's no problem.

Bruise   So the King took the mirror to the Prince.

Tattoo   Look at this! What d'you see, Prince?

Hands mirror to **Quiff**.

Quiff   Wicked!

Glitter   What is it?

Quiff   Colours and sparkly things.

Satchel   And what about your battle with the Dragon?

Quiff   Who cares?

Child claps his hands in approval.

Old Woman   Very good.

Bruise   The King went to the Princess and told her about the magic mirror.

Tattoo   All we've got to do is break off little bits when the Prince ain't looking. Soon there'll be no mirror. And … well, who knows? You might be able to care for him.

Bruise   You've forgotten something.

Tattoo   What?

Satchel   The warning.

Child whispers in **Old Woman's** *ear.*

Old Woman   Good boy. Not to look in the mirror.

Bruise   So, that night, Princess Glitter broke a tiny piece from the mirror and looked —

Glitter   Oh, wonderful.

Bruise   And then — a noise in the sky!

Tattoo   What's going on now?

Old Woman   A Dragon!

Bruise   More than one! Because, when the Prince had returned from killing the Dragon, he forgot about one thing. Guess what?

Child rushes to Bruise and whispers in her ear.

Bruise   Oh, clever boy! The nest!

Child whispers in her ear again.

Bruise   With eggs. Exactly! And now the Dragons have grown up and ...

Child sniffs loudly.

Bruise   They smell the roses.

Child flaps arms as if flying.

Bruise   They're coming to eat the garden.

Old Woman   Well done.

Bruise   The Dragons are coming.

Old Woman   The Dragons are coming.

Child runs around flapping arms.

Tattoo   Prince! Son! Do something! — Oh, stop looking in the mirror.

Quiff   Wicked!

Tattoo   Princess!

Glitter   Wonderful!

Tattoo   Wizard!

Satchel   I warned you.

Bruise   Before long there was no garden left. The Dragons ... oh, they ate everything.

*Child whispers in **Bruise's** ear.*

Bruise   And more?

*Child points at **Satchel**.*

Bruise   They ate Wizard satchel.

Quiff   Bad luck, Satch!

*Child points at **Glitter**.*

Bruise   And Princess Glitter.

Quiff   Ha! Ha!

*Child points at **Quiff**.*

Bruise   And Prince Quiff.

Quiff   I'm dead again! Help!

Bruise   And King Tattoo's eaten?

Child shakes head.

Bruise   Not the King?

*Child whispers in **Bruise's** ear.*

Bruise   The King lives on. He tells everyone the story. How he once had everything. And lost it. Because he wouldn't share his garden.

Old woman   And that's the end?

Child nods.

Old Woman   Who's got the mirror?

Glitter holds up the mirror.

Old Woman   You know what to do.

    Glitter puts mirror on fire.

Context of the play

The action of the play is set in a ruined house after an unspecified disaster
has taken place. In the house a young child, who seems to have been
abandoned, gets ready for bed. The other characters, six young people and an
elderly woman – who appear to have forgotten their real names – come
together in the devastated house, and to calm the child start to improvise
stories. Each character becomes the focus for a different story, and, as the play
progresses, the storytelling develops from narrative – storytelling – into
theatre.

This extract is taken from the middle of the play. Bruise, a 15-year-old girl (so
called because of the bruise on her leg), takes her turn to tell a story. At this
stage in the play the drama is constantly moving between dramatic action and
narration.

Introductory task

1. In your group, decide on a story that you all know well. Tell the story (or a
section of it) round the group with each person adding a few lines.

2. Tell the story a second time, with one of the group narrating while the rest of
the group enact particular moments. This may need a little organisation!

3. Tell the story again. For this final version, present it as a drama; allocate parts
to each member, and improvise the drama, using a straightforward storytelling style.

4. What are the differences between the three versions you have created?

Task 1

In the stage directions to the play, Philip Ridley writes:

Twinkling stars.
Ethereal moonlight reveals –

A ruined house; no ceiling, near-demolished walls, smashed windows, stairway. Several piles of
rubble. A big puddle.

Signs of family life are scattered everywhere; framed photographs, toys, etc. Also a bed, table, chairs. Everything damaged by some nameless catastrophe. In the moonlight this becomes a dreamscape of broken memory.

1. The style of the piece allows objects 'found' in the ruined building to be used as props. Make a list of all the objects mentioned in the extract. What other objects could be put to use in a similar way to enhance the story/drama?

2. Stage a section of the text in order to demonstrate how you might use these 'found' objects in an imaginative way.

Task 2

1. In small groups, design the set for the play. Read the extract for any clues it might give, then create a plan of the stage, and draw an 'artist's impression' sketch of the stage from the audience's perspective.

2. Compare the ideas that different groups have about a set for this play. Which are particularly effective?

Cultural references

What other stories, plays or films do you know that are set after a major disaster has happened? Why do you think writers are attracted to settings such as these? Why are we – as audiences – so fascinated by them?

Writing task

At first sight, the story enacted in this extract seems to be a fantasy about dragons and magic mirrors. Do you think that it could have a meaning beyond that? The setting of the play is 'post-apocalyptic' (this means that it takes place after an apocalypse – the end of the world). Bearing in mind this setting, does it have a moral message or stand as a warning?

Produce a short piece of writing attempting to explain the 'message' of this story.

After Juliet

Sharman McDonald

Characters in this extract

Benvolio	a Montague, Romeo's cousin
Valentine	a Montague, Mercutio's twin brother
Rosaline	a Capulet, Juliet's cousin

Plot summary

After the deaths of Romeo and Juliet, their families – the Montagues and the Capulets – are living on in a tense state of truce. Benvolio, Romeo's cousin and best friend, is in love with Rosaline, Juliet's cousin, but Rosaline is struggling to work through her feelings of anger and hurt.

In this extract, Benvolio and Valentine – twin brother of the dead Mercutio – are observing Rosaline at Juliet's grave.

Thunder and church bells.

The rain's pouring down.

Benvolio's *watching from the shadows with* **Valentine**.

In the distance, **Rosaline**.

Benvolio	She's coming back.
Valentine	There's better fish in the sea than ever came out of it.

Benvolio grabs him.

Benvolio	Do you call my love a fish, sir?
Valentine	Do I call your love a fish, sir?
Benvolio	Do you call my love a fish?
Valentine	I do call your love a fish.
Benvolio	Do you call her a fish, sir?
Valentine	I do call her a fish, sir.
	I do not call her a trout.
Benvolio	You do not call her a trout, sir?
Valentine	I do not call her a trout, sir.
	Do you crush my collar?
Benvolio	I do crush your collar, sir.
Valentine	Do you crush my new collar?
Benvolio	What kind of fish?
Valentine	What kind of fish?
Benvolio	What kind of fish, sir?
Valentine	A red snapper.

Benvolio   A red snapper?

Valentine   A red snapper.

Benvolio   That's a pretty kind of fish.

Valentine   It is a tasty fish.

Prettier than a pike.

Benvolio   Do you call my love a pike?

Valentine   I do call you a fool.

Throw your cat fish back in the pond.

And unhand my lace, Benvolio.

Misery provoked.

Benvolio   I haven't got her out of the pond yet.

She is a young carp.

Queen of fish, Valentine,

Who will not come to my hand

Though I tempt her with soft white bread.

And I tell her my hand is gentle.

Valentine   A carp?

Valentine pouches up his mouth and makes a fish face.

Benvolio   It was a metaphor.

Valentine   Fuck off.

Benvolio   I'm not asking you to love her.

Valentine   Don't go down this road, Benvolio.

Benvolio   Will I lose your friendship?

Valentine   For loving a Capulet?

Benvolio   Well?

Valentine   The Prince says hostilities are at an end.

Benvolio   What do you say?

Valentine   Can the Prince change the habits of a lifetime with a word?

Did his 'word' bring my brother back to life?

Do the dead live because an amnesty is called?

And if they don't live how can there be peace?

Where is Mercutio now?

There is such a silence

In the world

Since he has left it.

I was never alone

Not even in the womb.

For we were twin souls

Mercutio and me.

Now I am cut in half

My good part's gone.

His death sets my heart

To beat a tattoo of hate.

The Prince may speak his word.

May speak and speak.

He cannot change my heart beat.

I'll watch the girl with you in friendship.

Approach her and our friendship ends.

Benvolio At least it's wet.

Valentine Why?

Benvolio Hate cools in the rain.

Tears become invisible.

*The drummer hits the rim: points at **Valentine**.*

Valentine And yet it's close.

He whirrs a small electric hand fan into life.

The shadows hide them.

The rain patters down.

The drum sticks click.

***Rosaline** walks up to a pile of flowers in the corner of the piazza. She's holding a single lily. And an umbrella.*

Rosaline Your spirit haunts me, Juliet.

I see more of you dead

Than I did when you were alive;

***Valentine** splutters with laughter.*

The drummer whirls and points.

***Benvolio** puts his hand over his friend's mouth.*

That's a joke.

'More of you dead.'

She stamps her foot hard down as if knocking on the door of the grave.

Go on laugh.

And more of you alive

Than I wanted to.

Laugh. Laugh, go on.

Knocks again.

Come on, Juliet.

Benvolio *pulls* **Valentine** *deep into the shadows.*

We were hardly close as cousins.

You were too small, too pretty, too rich,

Too thin and too much loved for me to cope with.

'Spoilt' is the word that springs to mind.

Though I don't want to speak ill of the dead.

She touches the stamen of the lily. Yellow nicotine pollen stains her fingers. She rubs it in.

All a flower does is wither

It's the memories that stay for ever:

So they tell me.

So what do I recall of you?

Juliet, daddy's princess, rich,

Mummy's darling, quite a bitch.

You scratched my face once,

From here to here;

I have the scar. I have it yet.

You can see it quite clearly

In the sunlight;

A silver line.

You wanted my favourite doll.

And of course you got it.

For though I was scarred, you cried.

And your nurse swooped down

And took the moppet from me.

Spanked me hard for making you unhappy;

Gave my doll to you, her dearest baby.

Later you stole my best friend;

Wooed her with whispers;

Told her gossip's secrets;

Gave her trinkets, sweetmeats.

Later still, you took my love

And didn't know you'd done it;

Then having taken him

You let him die.

If you'd swallowed the friar's potion earlier

You would have wakened.

And my love would be alive.

None of this would have happened.

I know you, Juliet.

You hesitated, frightened.

Didn't take the stuff until the dawn.

Wakened too late in the tomb.

In the night I dream of Romeo.

He's reaching his arms out from the vault.

The poison has him in its hold.

He fills my nights with his longing for life.

Until I am afraid to go to sleep.

For though I love him still

I cannot soothe his pain.

If I could, I would

But it is not me he's reaching for.

So why, Juliet,

Should I spend my cash

On flowers for you?

Are you a saint

Simply because you were daft enough

To die for love?

Love?

A passing fancy,

No more nor less.

Tomorrow or tomorrow or tomorrow

You would have tired of him.

Like your fancy for the doll;

Once possessed, you left it in the rain;

Yesterday's fancy, mud in its hair,

Damp stained the dress I'd made for her.

> They think you brave to have taken your life

But you believed in immortality

Daddy's princess could not die.

She would be there at her own funeral

To watch the tears flow

And hear her praises sung.

 So you haunt me.

Don't turn away.

Listen. Listen.

What is it that you've brought about?

What trail does your fancy drag behind?

What punishments lie in your fancy's wake?

Listen, Juliet.

Come here. Come close.

Press your ear to the earth

So I know you're listening.

There's a trail going on.

Even now. In all solemnity.

Four lives hang in the balance

Forced by your selfish suicide

To take their chance

Standing at the mercy of the court.

They wait to see whether life or death

Is granted them by what we call justice.

It's a strange justice. Law meted out by the rich

Who measure their wisdom

By the weight of their gold;

As if riches bear witness to virtue.

You and I know they don't.

So four poor people are brought before the Prince

To see whether they live or die.

You brought this on them.

No feud wrought their trials.

Their misery is tribute

To your precocity.

Married. And at thirteen!

So. So. Sweet Coz.

Here. This is the last flower

You'll get from me.

Death flowers have the sweetest scent.

She casts the flower down. Shrugs.

That's that bit done.

She puts down the umbrella. Stands with her face up to the rain.

Benvolio   Some loves are for ever.

Valentine   Jealous of dead Juliet.

Oh Lord. Oh Lord.

These Capulets.

Love?

This is love.

A pile of rotting lilies.

Benvolio   They're still fresh on the top.

Valentine   Only you.

Benvolio   What?

Valentine   A pile of stinking lilies bathed in catpiss,

Only you would see the fresh ones on the top.

And love Rosaline whose heart's in the grave.

There are softer beds to lie on.

Than fair Rosaline's nail strewn cot.

Benvolio   I love because I love.

I can't say why I love.

I would take her in my arms,

Confess my love,

Ask for her clemency.

Change her name.

Valentine   She'd have you for breakfast.

That girl is the enemy.

She'd eat you up, suck on the bits

And after, lick her chops.

She's a hurt animal.

A cat that would attack the hand

That gentles it.

And bite it hard.

Princess of Cats.

She's a better man

Than Tybalt ever was

Or Petruchio ever shall be.

Give her a sword

She'd show you no mercy.

Though she has no need of a sword.

What woman does?

While the Prince has taken our weapons

He's left them theirs.

Benvolio What weapons?

Valentine Have you no sisters?

A woman's weapon is her tongue.

See her. See.

Conjoin with her.

You'll fight the oldest feud of all.

Not Montagues and Capulets.

Men and women Benvolio.

Men and women. There's a war.

Will never end by any decree

Of man, or Prince, Or God. Don't go near her.

Valentine mimes whipping out a sword. Mimes balancing it on the tips of his fingers by its point.

Benvolio There's no sword there.

Valentine I see a sword.

A Toledo steel.

My sword.

The hilt thirsty for my hand.

The blade starved of blood.

See it gleam in the light.

See it. See it.

He mimes throwing it up in the air, catching it again and sheathing it.

Now it's gone.

When the trial's over

And the guilty hung

I'll have my sword again.

Context of the play

Can two families who have hated each other for so long and lost so much, put aside their grievances and begin to build bridges? *After Juliet* attempts to answer this question. The dramatic action begins soon after Romeo and Juliet are placed in their tomb. The uneasy truce enforced by Prince Escalus seems unreal in the minds of the younger members of the warring clans. The trial of the Nurse, Friar Lawrence, Juliet's servant Peter and the Apothecary forms a backdrop to the play as society attempts to punish those held responsible for the young lovers' deaths.

The play mirrors some of the themes framed in *Romeo and Juliet* – there is love across a divide, as Benvolio attempts to capture the heart of Rosaline, Juliet's cousin and one-time object of Romeo's affections. Rosaline, an incidental character in Shakespeare's play, takes a central role in *After Juliet*. It is through her that themes of conflict, forgiveness, grief, revenge and identity are explored. The unfolding narrative has a claustrophobic, dream-like quality, enhanced by the presence of the controlling, voiceless figure of the Drummer.

In this extract Benvolio and Valentine spy upon Rosaline laying flowers at Juliet's tomb. Valentine is angered by Benvolio's affections towards Rosaline. Rosaline reflects upon her relationship with Juliet and it becomes clear whom she blames for Romeo's death.

Introductory task

1. In small groups, remind yourselves of the outcome of Shakespeare's *Romeo and Juliet*. Read the final few pages of the play. The heads of the families decide that a statue or memorial should be built to commemorate the tragedy. Discuss and decide what this memorial might look like.

2. Form two groups – Capulets and Montagues. Stand facing each other and imagine the memorial is between you. Choose a character from *After Juliet* or from *Romeo and Juliet* and devise a short speech that gives your reaction to the memorial, the past events and your hopes for the future.

3. Experiment with different ways of presenting this drama – exploring words and phrases, vocal techniques and different voice qualities. Introduce stylized or repeated gesture or movement to represent the conflict between the

families and suggest a dream-like quality. Can your group find a way of expressing the fact that this feud is far from over?

Task 1

1. In small groups, read Act 1 Scene 1 of *Romeo and Juliet*, up to Tybalt's entrance. Are there any similarities between this scene and the opening sequence of the extract, between Benvolio and Valentine?

2. Return to the *After Juliet* extract. Benvolio and Valentine are friends. How do you think this section of dialogue should be acted out? Experiment with different tempos and rhythms. Are they being serious or is there humour in the word play and physical action? How would you develop that humour?

Task 2

1. The three characters in this section of the play all have very different viewpoints. In your group, identify what these points of view are. Ironically, Rosaline and Valentine share a common attitude towards the feud. What do you think that is?

2. In your group assign the role of Rosaline to a volunteer. Place a chair in the middle of the group and conduct a hot-seating session where the actor playing Rosaline answers questions in role. Take some cues from her long speech as to what to explore – who does she blame for Romeo's death, what does she feel about the trial, what are her hopes for the future, what does she feel towards Benvolio?

3. Return to the extract, and choose a section from Rosaline's monologue that you think might provoke a reaction in both Valentine and Benvolio as they secretly watch. Explore different ways of staging this section so that the two men's reactions are apparent and build up the dramatic tension.

Task 3

In your group, read through the first half of Rosaline's monologue. Identify incidents from Rosaline's past that shaped her relationships in later life. What sort of picture does Rosaline paint of her cousin? Choose a section of text that has two or three such descriptions. Devise a drama that has Rosaline's monologue as its focus and central strand, but cross-cuts to brief re-enactments of Rosaline's childhood and recent history. Decide whether the actor reading Rosaline's part steps into these scenes or whether another actor plays the younger Rosaline. Explore different ways of staging your drama – use levels or define areas by light to show the flashback sequences.

Cultural references

Consider communities you are aware of that are divided along political, religious, ethnic or social grounds. Think globally and historically. Sometimes physical barriers are put up to separate warring sections of these communities. Try to find images of the 'peace walls' in Northern Ireland. How else do communities mark out their identity and territory? Some barriers are not physical, but are equally divisive – history, wealth, class, gender and ethnicity can create significant barriers between groups of people.

Written task

Write a series of notes that will help an actor preparing Rosaline's long monologue. Indicate how an actor might highlight contrasts in the speech and how these might be presented in performance. Consider voice, tone, stillness and silences, body language, movement and posture. Are the lines directed at the audience, or are they externalized inner thoughts? How would an actor show this? Say what you think the audience should learn about Rosaline by the end of the speech.

Acknowledgements

We are grateful for permission to reprint extracts from the following copyright material:

Steven Berkoff: adaptation of Franz Kafka: *Metamorphosis* (Amber Lane Press, 1981, 1988), copyright © Steven Berkoff 1981, reprinted by permission of the publishers. For performing rights please apply to Rosica Colin Ltd, 1 Clareville Grove Mews, London SW7 5AH.

Bertolt Brecht: *The Resistable Rise of Arturo Ui* translated by Ralph Manheim (Methuen, 1976), reprinted by permission of Methuen Publishing Ltd. For performing rights please apply to Samuel French Ltd, www.samuelfrench-london.co.uk.

Tanika Gupta: adaptation of Harold Brighouse: *Hobson's Choice* (Oberon, 2003), reprinted by permission of the publisher. For performing rights please apply to The Agency (London) Ltd, 24 Pottery Lane, London W11 4LZ.

Ayub Khan-Din: *East is East* (Nick Hern Books, 1997), copyright © 1996, 1997 Ayub Khan-Din, reprinted by permission of the publisher: www.nickhern-book.co.uk. For performing rights please apply to info@nickhernbooks.demon.co.uk.

Sharman Macdonald: *After Juliet* (Stanley Thornes, 1999), reprinted by permission of Nelson Thornes. For performing rights please apply to the PFD Group, Drury House, 34-43 Russell Street, London WC2B 5HA.

Richard Norton-Taylor: *The Colour of Justice* (Oberon, 1999), reprinted by permission of the publisher. For performing rights please apply to Oberon Books, 521 Caledonian Road, London N7 9RH.

Bernard Pomerance: *The Elephant Man* (Samuel French Inc, 1979), copyright © Bernard Pomerance 1979, reprinted by permission of Alan Brodie Representation Ltd. For performing rights please apply to Alan Brodie Representation, 6th Floor, Fairgate House, 78 New Oxford Street, London WC1A 1HB, info@alanbrodie.com.

Philip Ridley: *Brokenville* (Faber/Stanley Thornes, 2001), reprinted by permission of Nelson Thornes. For performing rights please apply to The Rod Hall Agency Ltd, 6th Floor, Fairgate House, 78 New Oxford Street, London WC1A 1HB.

August Strindberg: *Miss Julie* translated by Helen Cooper (Methuen, 1992), translation copyright © Helen Cooper 1992, reprinted by permission of Methuen Publishing Ltd. For performing rights please apply to Judy Daish Associates Ltd, 2 St Charles Place, London W10 6EG. All Rights reserved.

Mark Wheeller: *Too Much Punch for Judy* (IAS 1988/dbda 1999), reprinted by permission of MBA Literary Agents Ltd. For more details on the playwright and his other work see Mark Wheeller's website: www.amdram.co.uk/wheellerplays. For a copy of the full script please contact dbda, Pin Point, 1-2 Rosslyn Crescent, Harrow, Middlesex HA1 2SB, Tel: 0870 333 7771, Fax: 0870 333 7772, email: dbda@dbda.co.uk; or Maverick Musicals, 89 Bergann Road, Maleny, QLD 4522, Australia. Tel/Fax: +617 5494 4007, email: helen@mavmuse.com, www.mavmuse.com. For performing rights please apply to Sophie Gorell Barnes at MBA LIterary Agents Ltd, 62 Grafton Way, London W1T 5DW, Tel: 020 7387 2076, Fax: 020 7387 2042, email: sophie@mbalit.co.uk, www.mbalit.co.uk.